Congressional
Communication

Congressional Communication

Content & Consequences

Daniel Lipinski

University of Michigan Press
Ann Arbor

Copyright © by the University of Michigan 2004
All rights reserved
Published in the United States of America by
The University of Michigan Press
Manufactured in the United States of America
⊚ Printed on acid-free paper

2007 2006 2005 2004   4 3 2 1

No part of this publication may be reproduced,
stored in a retrieval system,
or transmitted in any form or by any means,
electronic, mechanical, or otherwise,
without the written permission of the publisher.

A CIP catalog record for this book is available from the British Library.

Library of Congress Cataloging-in-Publication Data

Lipinski, Daniel.
Congressional communication : content and consequences /
Daniel Lipinski.
    p.   cm.
Includes bibliographical references and index.
ISBN 0-472-03019-1 (pbk. : alk. paper)
1. United States. Congress—Constituent communication.
2. Communication in politics—United States. I. Title.
JK1131.L57   2004
328.73'0731—dc22   2004004963

*This book is dedicated to my parents,
William and RoseMarie Lipinski,
whose innumerable sacrifices gave me
the opportunities to learn, grow,
and begin to fulfill
the gifts God has given me.*

ACKNOWLEDGMENTS

Some time has passed since I wrote the acknowledgments for this project when it was a doctoral dissertation, but I need to begin this book by repeating those thanks because they will never be enough.

Many thanks go to those colleagues who provided suggestions, and—most importantly—friendship and encouragement, down the long road of graduate school. I would most like to thank John Rattliff, Danielle Vinson, Karen Kedrowski, Zoe Oxley, and Mark Berger. Troy Dostert and Jim Battista deserve thanks for serving as trustworthy research assistants as well as valuable colleagues in graduate school. And I would also like to thank all my friends at the Duke Catholic Student Center who encouraged me in my pursuit of this long sought-after goal while never letting me lose sight of what I ultimately strive for.

Many members of Congress and their staffs, all of whom will go unnamed to protect the anonymity of their contributions, aided me in this research. I am deeply indebted to these people for their opinions and insights. Two people on Capitol Hill whom I can publicly thank are Jack Dail and Karen Buehler at the House Franking Commission.

My dissertation committee deserves many thanks for their aid both during the dissertation phase and afterward. Bill Bianco was especially influential in the development of some of the important insights in this book. John Aldrich inspired and guided me from my first class at Duke through the completion of this book. David Paletz supplied me with many insights and my first professional opportunities. John Brehm helped me through many methodological questions. In addition I would like to thank David Price for the advice and insights he provided before being called to serve in Congress. I would also like to thank R. Michael Alvarez and Paul Gronke for providing important data and ideas that helped shape chapter 5.

A National Science Foundation Dissertation Improvement Grant (SBER-9520169) aided me in my research for this project.

Acknowledgments

There are many more people I would like to thank for their assistance in the development of this book. Richard Fenno provided numerous valuable insights throughout the entire development of the project. David Brady, John Hibbing, and Glen Parker gave helpful advice as I worked on the revisions. I would also like to thank Paul Herrnson and the Center for American Politics and Citizenship at the University of Maryland for support during a summer of book revisions.

I would like to thank my wife, Judy, for all the support and encouragement as I completed the revisions for this book. Judy was not with me when this project started, and it is possible that I would have completed this book without her; but without Judy I know that my life would not be filled with the joy we now share.

This book is dedicated to my parents, William and RoseMarie Lipinski, who have given me countless opportunities to learn and grow. Growing up in a middle-class bungalow in ethnic Chicago, they promised me that they would support me through all of my schooling (although I don't think they imagined how many years it could be). This book is a token of my appreciation for all the love and support that they have given me that I will never be able to repay.

Without the help of all of these people, completion of this book would not have been possible. They contributed much to this book, but I remain responsible for any errors or shortcomings.

CONTENTS

List of Tables   xi

Chapter 1.   *Studying Congressional Communication*   1

Chapter 2.   *Measuring Members' Messages with Mail*   9

I. CONTENT

Chapter 3.   *Members' Messages Regarding Congress*   19

Chapter 4.   *Running with the Party*   47

II. CONSEQUENCES

Chapter 5.   *Members' Success in Communicating Information to Constituents*   73

Chapter 6.   *The Electoral Impact of Members' Messages*   89

Chapter 7.   *A New View of Members' Behavior and the Representative-Constituent Connection*   101

Appendixes   111
Notes   125
Bibliography   135
Index   141

LIST OF TABLES

1. Members Who Sent Any Messages about Congressional Performance — 39
2. Members Sending Positive Messages, Negative Messages, No Messages, and Mixed Messages — 41
3. Members Sending Positive and Negative Messages by Party — 42
4. Members Sending Positive and Negative Messages about Policies and Processes by Party — 44
5. Members Sending Positive and Negative Messages by Type of Mail — 45
6. Factors Affecting the Probability of Sending Negative Messages, No Messages, or Positive Messages in All Mail — 51
7. Factors Affecting the Probability of Sending Negative Messages, No Messages, or Positive Messages in Districtwide Mail — 53
8. Factors Affecting the Probability of Sending Negative Messages, No Messages, or Positive Messages in Targeted Mail — 54
9. Factors Affecting the Probability of Sending Negative Messages, No Messages, or Positive Messages about Policies — 55
10. Factors Affecting the Probability of Sending Negative Messages, No Messages, or Positive Messages about Processes — 56
11. Factors Affecting the Probability of Sending Negative Messages, No Messages, or Positive Messages about Processes, with Cohort Variable — 59
12. Members Who Publicized Vote for Each Level of Media Market Congruence — 83

List of Tables

13. Factors Affecting Respondents' Perceptual Accuracy of Their Representative's Vote on the Persian Gulf War Use of Force Resolution — 84
14. Factors Affecting Respondents' Perceptual Accuracy of Their Representative's Vote on the 1993 Budget-Reconciliation Conference Report, Democratic Representatives Only — 87
15. Factors Affecting Probability of Defeat in 1994 — 96
16. Probability of Defeat by Loyalty Score — 97

1 STUDYING CONGRESSIONAL COMMUNICATION

When communicating with constituents, every politician is thinking strategically; if he says he's not he is lying.
—Veteran Capitol Hill staff member

THE IMPORTANCE OF CONGRESSIONAL COMMUNICATION

In recent decades congressional scholars have developed a much better understanding of the representative-constituent connection by taking a broader view of representation. Instead of focusing strictly on the congruence of representatives' roll call votes with the preferences of their constituents, attention has been given to the wide variety of activities engaged in by members that both reflect and affect their bonds with constituents (for examples, see Mayhew 1974a; Fiorina, esp. 1979; Fenno, esp. 1978; Parker 1986). In the move away from studying representation in terms of specific votes, the shift in focus to members' communication with constituents was critical. If the representational relationship is significantly affected by public perceptions, we must know what legislators are doing strategically to shape constituents' views and the impact that these actions are having. In this book I provide rich, systematic measures of the content of the messages sent by members of the U.S. House of Representatives to their constituents and then demonstrate the consequences of this communication, focusing specifically on evaluations of congressional performance. My findings challenge the conventional wisdom that members "run against Congress" and provide valuable support for theories claiming the importance of congressional parties.

While congressional scholars have only recently given more attention to communication from representatives to constituents, democratic theorists have long recognized it as an important component of representation. Thomas Jefferson professed that members had both a right and a duty to communicate with constituents. When a grand jury in Virginia charged that one congressman's correspondence with his constituents was a threat to the government, Jefferson defended him "as a good and dutiful representative, [who] was in the habit of corresponding with many of his constituents and communicating to us . . . information of the public proceedings" (1955, 164). Permeating democratic theory is the idea that the people, through frequent elections, are the source of authority for government and the primary safeguard against its abuses. Constituents need information to fulfill their responsibilities in the system and to protect their own interests; therefore they need sources of such data.

Surveys indicate the importance that the public places on members providing them with information. In the 1978 American National Election Study (ANES) respondents said that the number one job of House members should be "keeping in touch with the people about what government is doing." The potential impact of members' direct communication is especially significant because the news media do not provide a large amount of information about Congress or individual representatives. Congress and its members garner little attention on either the national (Davis 1987; Cook 1989) or local levels (Vinson 2002). Since constituents are often left with little information, they have to rely on the communication that comes directly from their representatives.

"RUNNING AGAINST CONGRESS"

But members' communication cannot be understood as motivated purely by a desire to serve their duty. As Madison stated in *Federalist 52*, the House of Representatives was designed to "have an immediate dependence on, and an intimate sympathy with, the people" (1987, 323–24). The fact that elections take place every two years provides representatives with a strong incentive to send self-interested messages designed to build the support of constituents. Mayhew (1974a) posited members as single-minded seekers of reelection and claimed that this goal leads them to communicate messages that serve three purposes: advertising, credit claiming, and position taking. All of these messages are strategically designed to be self-promotional. Many of our perceptions of congressional communication come from Richard Fenno's observational study of eighteen representatives described in *Home Style* (1978). Fenno assumed that members have three goals: reelection, good public policy, and power (1973). However, "for most members of Congress most of the time, [the] electoral goal is primary" (1978, 31). In pursuit of reelection a member develops a "home style" chosen to build the trust of constituents. Two of the three activities that compose a "home style" directly involve communication: "presentation of self" and "explanation of Washington activities."[1]

Fenno's unique research in *Home Style* revealed many different aspects of representatives' relationships with their constituents. But while following representatives as they interacted with constituents in their districts he was particularly surprised by one consistent message he heard. Fenno summarized this discovery with a statement that has become one of the most frequently quoted dicta in congressional studies: "members of Congress run *for* Congress by running *against* Congress" (1978, 168).[2] A representative was said to do this by "differentiating himself or herself from the others in Congress, attacking Congress as an institution, and portraying himself or herself as a fighter against its manifest shortcomings" (168). Although Fenno did not explicitly state the claim, he implied that all members had the same incentives to make this behavior a part of their home style.

> Nothing . . . had prepared me to discover that each member of Congress polishes his or her individual reputation at the expense of the institutional reputation of Congress. . . . [T]he members' process of differentiating themselves from the Congress as a whole only served, directly or indirectly, to downgrade the Congress. (164)

Soon thereafter, Cook's (1979) analysis of survey data led him to conclude that he had found "some empirical corroboration for Fenno's suggestions that members of Congress win reelection by running against the institution of Congress" (48). Thus the evidence suggested that this was a common, dominant strategy that produced the intended positive electoral results for members.

The belief that members "run against Congress" was quickly embraced and is now considered conventional wisdom. The widespread acceptance and impact can be seen in various types of work, from articles exploring public attitudes toward Congress (for example, see Patterson and Caldeira 1990), to popular textbooks about the institution (see Davidson and Oleszek 2003), to introductory American government course books (see Fiorina and Peterson 2003). This notion has a number of implications for our understanding of Congress. In regard to members' behavioral motivations, it suggests that all representatives—no matter their personal partisanship, constituents' partisanship, electoral context, or other environmental factors—have incentives that motivate them to send messages denigrating the institution. One of the most important implications relates to the controversial congressional party government theories that suggest that members will rhetorically support and run with their parties when seeking reelection (see esp. Cox and McCubbins 1993). If partisanship is not important in shaping the messages legislators send, then the theories purporting the importance of parties are undermined.

IMPLICATIONS OF "RUNNING AGAINST CONGRESS"

This belief concerning what members communicate about the institution also has significant ramifications for the representative-constituent relationship. If "running against Congress" is an ongoing electoral strategy, members must believe that this is an effective method of building constituents' trust. We have some limited evidence suggesting that this has been true (Cook 1979), but if it is such a prevalent strategy it is certainly worth more careful empirical study. After all, in order to be an effective strategy, members must be communicating this message, constituents must be receiving it and accepting it as intended by legislators, and the information must be persuasive in shaping votes. While most literature examining the content of members' communication at least implicitly assumes that this behavior accomplishes its goals, there is little empirical evidence demonstrating any impact, much less a significant effect on elections.

There is one more widely believed (though not necessary) implication of the "running against Congress" dictum in regard to the effect on public views of the institution. If members are continually denigrating Congress when they communicate with their constituents they could be influencing public views of the institution. One of the best-known and enduring aspects of the public's relationship with Congress is the low approval rating that the institution historically receives in opinion polls (Durr, Gilmour, and Wolbrecht 1997; Parker 1981; Patterson and Magleby 1992).[3] The assumption that members' consistently negative messages concerning Congress were at least partially responsible for the institution's low approval ratings also became accepted in congressional studies (see Fenno 1975; Cook 1979). Thus the reputation of the institution (and perhaps its legitimacy), at least in the eyes of congressional scholars, is impacted when members send these negative messages.

Despite the critical implications of this belief for our understanding of many different aspects of Congress, congressional scholars have failed to take a second look at whether members *are* "running against Congress." While *Home Style* will always remain one of the most important works on the representative-constituent relationship (and probably *the* most significant work), we must take into account that the findings were based on limited observations made more than twenty-five years ago. But the need for a new examination of congressional communication, especially members' messages regarding the performance of the institution, goes beyond these reasons. Recent claims in congressional literature prompt us to question whether all members have incentives for "running against Congress." Most significantly, party government theories say that majority party representatives grant their leadership important powers that can be used to encourage and discipline reluctant members to act in ways that promote the passage of partisan legislation (Rohde 1991; Cox and McCubbins 1993; Sinclair 1995, 1999; Aldrich and Rohde 1998). The purpose is both to pass a legislative agenda favored by most party members and to build the party's reputation with the public.[4] But reputations are not shaped only by actions; they can be influenced by the messages received by the public. This suggests that members in the majority have an incentive to praise their party when they communicate with the public in order to build favorable perceptions of the way the institution is being managed. Thus these theories suggest that majority party members actually have an electoral incentive to be positive about institutional performance in order to build their party's record. "Running against Congress" would serve to harm public perceptions of the party that controls the institution.

A new examination of representatives' messages about Congress would not only test the conventional wisdom and all its implications, but it also would be a unique check of the predictions of party government theories in the electoral arena. If this study confirmed Fenno's finding we could confidently continue to hold and work with the belief that members "run against Congress" and all that this suggests about congressional representation. In addition, we would have even stronger evidence corroborating Krehbiel's anecdotal data from 1994 and 1996 rejecting the party government prediction (1998). However, if we find that members are not all running against Congress, and further that members' messages are significantly impacted by partisanship, we have evidence supporting party government theories in the arena of electoral campaigning.

STUDYING THE IMPACT OF COMMUNICATION

Studying the messages sent by representatives even without any evidence that they have an impact would still be worthwhile for improving our understanding of members' behavior. But by testing the impact we will better understand the consequences of this communication. In order to have any effect messages first have to be received and remembered by the intended recipient. There is only scant empirical evidence that members have the ability to communicate successfully with constituents. Jacobson (2001) demonstrated that various forms of contact that members make with constituents can affect general public perceptions. Cover and Brumberg (1982) found that mailing nonpolitical, practical information to constituents can cause at least a short-term improvement in a representative's evaluations. But no studies have examined the extent to which members can successfully communicate specific pieces of information or the impact that certain messages have on reelection.

Ideally we could measure whether or not constituents have received and accepted their representative's messages about congressional performance and then test the impact that this has on voting. Unfortunately this is not possible with the available data and methods. Therefore I devised two separate tests of members' communication capabilities. First, I tested whether members can successfully communicate a particular piece of information crucial to the representative-constituent connection—the position they have taken on specific votes. Because votes are discrete pieces of information rather than opinions shaped by countless sources over a boundless time period, it is easier to measure members' impact on their constituents' knowledge of these. Using individual-level data and a previously formulated model controlling for other factors affecting the likelihood of knowing a representative's vote, we can measure the degree to which members can successfully communicate chosen information to their constituents.

Next, I studied whether members' messages about congressional performance could have an effect on their electoral chances. No matter what messages are being sent, congressional scholars would agree that the main purpose of this communication is to increase the likelihood of winning reelection. In order to test the success of this strategy I looked at macrolevel data from the 1994 elections to see whether members' messages evaluating congressional performance had a significant impact on whether they won or lost reelection.

One reason that the content of members' communication with their constituents has been largely ignored since *Home Style* is the difficulty of either reproducing Fenno's demanding observational study or developing an alternative method for examining members' messages. Each member of Congress has his own style in regard to not only his message content but also his communication methods. Since members face different constraints and opportunities they utilize varying methods that make it difficult to find a common measure of content that is realistically available for analysis. In order to overcome this obstacle I conducted a content analysis on all the official mass mailings sent by representatives to their constituents in 100 randomly selected districts between 1991 and 1995. The most common form of this type of mail is the newsletter, sent either to all constituents or to targeted groups based on issue interest or geography. The messages contained in mailings provide a good proxy for those sent by members in all forms of communication.

PLAN OF THE BOOK

The next chapter continues the discussion of mass mailings and the other data that were used for this study. I define what mass mailings are and how they were gathered for this study and I explain why mail content serves as an excellent proxy for the messages members send through all methods of communication. Then I discuss how representatives utilize these as an integral part of their communication strategies. I also describe how the surveys and interviews of representatives and their staffs were conducted in order to add depth to the empirical data.

Part I analyzes the content of members' messages about congressional performance and explains the variations in behavior. Chapter 3 begins with a review of the literature that has argued that members' incentives cause them to "run against Congress." Next I explain why members today may have differing incentives that encourage some, especially those in the majority, to send positive messages. I focus extensively on the theories of congressional party government propounded since the early 1990s. I then use the results from my survey to explore representatives' views of their behavioral incentives and their opinions about the impact of sending positive or negative messages about the institution. After giving examples of what judgments of congressional performance look like in mass mailings, I reveal that members of Congress do *not* all "run against Congress." Contrary to conventional wisdom there is considerable variance among members in the types of messages they communicate, with many being positive about Congress. The raw data suggest partisanship has a significant impact on this behavior, but what factors can be shown to explain the variance? This is the question I address in the next chapter.

In chapter 4 I demonstrate that when controlling for other factors—district partisanship, electoral security, seniority, and winning percentage on key votes—a representative's membership in the majority or minority party is the most significant predictor of the messages he will send about Congress. Members of both parties communicate positive or negative messages about Congress as a proxy for the majority party's record of performance running the institution. This results in members of the majority "running with Congress" while those in the minority "run against Congress." This is true even after control of the House switched parties in 1995. This finding supports party government theories that predict members will support and run on their party record during the permanent campaign for reelection. In addition, by examining targeted mail separately from mail sent to all constituents I am able to show that members' messages do not deviate even when they are addressing specific groups in their district. I also study how representatives use messages about policies and processes differently, but partisanship still remains the most important predictor of communication behavior.

Part II turns to studying the consequences of members' communication. Chapter 5 shows that members who put forth the effort to advertise their positions on two high-salience issues (the 1991 Persian Gulf War Use of Force Resolution and the 1993 Budget-Reconciliation Conference Report) were able to improve significantly the ability of their constituents to correctly state their votes in a survey. This demonstrates that members have a significant ability to communicate successfully their chosen messages to constituents. In addition, this finding shows that the messages recorded in mass mailings are meaningful measures of the content of members' communication.

In chapter 6 I examine the electoral impact of members' messages about congressional performance. Specifically I look at how the level of institutional loyalty displayed by a member in his judgments of Congress affected his probability of reelection in 1994. Members' messages to their constituents have been largely ignored in explanations of electoral results, but they are very important in helping to explain the surprising results of the 1994 congressional elections. The results reveal that Democrats who ran on their party record by making positive statements about congressional performance were more likely to *lose* than those who did not send such messages. This shows that constituents do not take the information that they receive from their representatives at face value, but instead filter it through their own perceptions. While Democrats wanted to impact views of the institution, it was voters' views of their representative that were shaped by these messages.

In chapter 7 I conclude by exploring the implications that these findings have for our understanding of congressional communication behavior and the representative-constituent connection.

2 MEASURING MEMBERS' MESSAGES WITH MAIL

> *Our number one priority always will be the people of Brookhaven, Smithtown, and the East End.*
>
> *Our number one priority always will be the people of Smithtown, Brookhaven, and the East End.*
>
> *Our number one priority always will be the people of the East End towns Southhampton, Riverhead, Southold, East Hampton, Shelter Island—and of course the towns of Brookhaven and Smithtown.*
>
> —Opening sentence in Mike Forbes's (R-NY) December 1995 newsletter strategically targeted and adapted to three different geographic areas in his district

Conducting a good examination of the messages that members of Congress are sending to their constituents has been hampered by the difficulty of finding a good, systematic method of measurement. Part of the reason Richard Fenno's observational study in *Home Style* was extraordinary was that it required significant time, resources, and access to gather the data. Even more remarkable was Fenno's keen ability to systematize his observations and produce important theoretical findings. The method I chose for studying members' messages was to conduct a content analysis of franked mass mailings. A mass mailing is defined as "any mailing of newsletters or other pieces of mail with substantially identical content . . . totaling more than 500 pieces during one session (year) of Congress."[1] In this chapter I explain the reasons why the content of mass mailings serve as an excellent proxy for all of a member's communication with constituents.

ADVANTAGES OF ANALYZING MAIL

There are a number of ways in which members communicate with constituents, including mediated methods (e.g., television, radio, and newspapers) and direct methods (e.g., personal appearances, websites, and mail). Members' abilities to communicate through the mass media vary significantly. A representative's relations with local journalists have an impact on the amount and favorability of coverage that she receives. For example, Tidmarch and Pitney (1985) conducted a study of ten local newspapers and found a number of different relationships between members and the news media ranging from symbiotic to conflictual. Stronger and more positive connections improve the likelihood of the representative receiving the type of coverage she desires. In addition, the level of geographic congruence between a district and its media markets affects the amount of coverage a representative receives. The fewer representatives there are to cover in a media market, the more likely each one is to be reported on by the local news media. In addition, the more people in a market who are represented by a particular member, the greater the likelihood that that individual legislator receives coverage.[2] These conditions result in representatives receiving widely varying amounts of news coverage regardless of their efforts. Most important, local news media provide little coverage of most representatives (Vinson 2002). Therefore any analysis of media coverage will not provide an accurate measure of the messages that members are attempting to communicate.

Because of the problems associated with studying mediated communication, it is essential to examine direct methods. While use of the internet is expanding rapidly, for most members of Congress electronic communication is still not a reliable method for delivering messages to all constituents. The extent to which members use websites to communicate still varies significantly, depending on the internet savvy of constituents and the representative. The information contained on many of these sites is often out-of-date, demonstrating the lack of attention paid to this medium as a critical communication tool.

A more ubiquitous means of direct communication is mail. All members are given the same resources to prepare and send mail to their constituents. In an extensive study of members' communication, Cook found that mass mailings are "the most popular of direct communication tactics" (1989, 98). While examining mail is not a common way to measure members' communication, the method has been utilized in previous research. Yiannakis (1982) looked at the content of newsletters (along with press releases) to analyze members' messages that stake out issue positions, claim credit, and advertise their names. Canon used newsletters (and press releases) to study representation because he claims that they "are the best possible sources for understanding the messages that members want to convey to their constituents" (1999, 215). Mailings probably have not been used more widely in congressional research because they are often difficult to collect and time-consuming to analyze.

Analyzing mail has many advantages over observing members' direct interactions with constituents. This method makes it easier to collect and analyze messages systematically, facilitates the use of a large data set containing easily comparable observations, and minimizes the problem of coding errors by allowing an intercoder reliability check. All of the mailings sent in 100 randomly selected congressional districts between 1991 and 1995 were analyzed.[3] This time span provides significant variance in a number of important factors including partisan control of Congress and the White House. In order to collect copies of the mailings I bypassed individual congressional offices and went directly to the Commission on Congressional Mailing Standards (better known as the Franking Commission).[4] The commission is required to approve the content of all franked mass mailings and keep a copy on file. This meant that I had access to every piece of mail sent by the representatives in the sample, eliminating the problem of response bias.[5]

Another advantage of this method is that there is no disparity among members in their abilities to deliver messages through this medium, unlike news media access. Mass mailings are sent to constituents using the congressional frank that allows members of Congress to send mail with their signature instead of a postage stamp. Use of the frank dates back to the First Continental Congress in 1775, but even with great advances in technology, sending franked mail is still a widely used method of communication.[6] The frank does not mean that representatives have unlimited mailing privileges, but each member is allotted a specific amount of money for sending franked mail.[7] Thus every office has similar resources for the creation and dissemination of mailings. While some members do not communicate with constituents through mass mailings, most choose to do so.[8] As I will demonstrate in chapter 3, about three-quarters of representatives utilize them to send messages to their constituents concerning Congress's performance.

The House Franking Commission must approve any mass mailing that is sent out with the frank. This is done to make sure that the mailings that are produced and sent with government funds are being used only for official purposes. Congressional offices must adhere to certain rules and regulations affecting the content of a mass mailing in order to be reimbursed for the costs of printing and postage.[9] These rules do not have a significant impact on members' messages evaluating the performance of the institution. There are imprecise rules that limit the blatant use of partisanship for political purposes, but these are vague enough to permit a large amount of flexibility. The commission is evenly divided between Democratic and Republican representatives to eliminate partisanship as a factor influencing how the regulations are applied. In order for any piece of mail to be certified as frankable one staff member from each party must agree that it complies with the rules.

The amount of direct input into the content of the mail that each member exercises varies significantly. Some members have no hand in the creation of mailings, others provide general directions including themes for particular articles or other directions for the content, and a few members write every word of their mass mailings.[10] But no matter how much of a direct contribution the member makes to his mailings there is no question that they reflect the strategic messages he wants to communicate. In general, no piece of mail—including letters going to only one constituent—can be sent out of an office without the approval of the member or the chief of staff (or in some cases the press secretary, when that position is one of the top two in the office). This ensures that all mail communicates ideas consistent with the member's views and political objectives and is consistent with messages being sent through all modes of communication.

In addition to the data collected through the content analysis of mailings, I conducted a survey of one-fifth of the House (86 representatives) during the 105th Congress (late 1997 through early 1998).[11] The survey was designed to provide a better understanding of the general strategies behind the use of mailings, what representatives see as their incentives in regard to sending messages about congressional performance and their vote stances, and party help with communication.[12] It is always essential to keep in mind that members are giving explanations of explanations; however, the survey respondents were guaranteed anonymity to encourage candid responses.[13] After completing the examination of the data gathered from the mailings, I interviewed 22 members of Congress (11 Republicans and 11 Democrats) and 20 congressional staff members (again evenly split between Democrats and Republicans) who are responsible for producing newsletters. Just as with the surveys, all of these interviews were conducted with an assurance of anonymity for the interviewees.

Surveys of members and interviews with members and staff also revealed wide agreement that the same messages are sent in mass mailings as are conveyed in personal appearances, media coverage, and all other forms of communication with constituents. Eighty percent of the members surveyed indicated that they send the "same messages" in all forms of communication, and when I include those who said they send "similar messages" this jumps to 94 percent. One member explained the reason for this by saying, "The judgment on salience [of issues] is likely to carry through whether the medium is personal appearance, town hall meeting, mass media, etc." That is, if a member believes a message is strategically important enough to disseminate in some other form of communication he will also want to discuss it in a mass mailing. A staff member who serves as communication director told me that one of his jobs is to make sure that in every medium of communication—mailings, press releases, public appearances, floor statements—the "representatives' language is identical." This may be an extreme case, but it points out the importance of sending a consistent message. Since the purpose of members' communication is to build trust with constituents they do not want to engage in behavior that would threaten this relationship. There are few actions that will undermine trust more quickly than to be caught sending inconsistent messages.

It is important to consider that these survey and interview responses may be shaped by strategic calculation. After all, members (and their staffs) may consider it risky to admit that they are sending different messages to different constituents. While this book does not include a direct comparison of messages sent through all of the various methods of communication, chapter 5 contains an important test of using the content of mailings as a proxy for members' messages. In examining whether members can successfully communicate to their constituents the votes that they cast, I use mailings to measure whether members attempted to communicate their stances on these votes. In showing that members do have the ability to communicate this information to their constituents, I also demonstrate the usefulness of mass mailings for measuring all the messages that members are communicating to their constituents.

DISTRICTWIDE AND TARGETED COMMUNICATION

It is important to understand the two types of mass mailings. Districtwide (or general audience) mail is sent to all households in the district, and targeted mail is only disseminated to specific addresses or within certain geographic locations. My survey indicates that 69 percent of representatives send at least one districtwide mass mailing to their constituents in a typical year, and about one-third of these legislators send three or more.[14] Districtwide mass mailings are often in the form of newsletters that are four to eight pages in length. Newsletters are ordinarily in a newspaper format with a variety of articles and pictures addressing different topics.[15]

There are generally two forms of targeted mail: the newsletter and the personally addressed letter. Two-thirds of members say that they usually send at least one targeted mass mailing each year.[16] There are a few different ways in which mail can be targeted. One method is to send a mailing to all households within a specific geographic area that can be isolated through use of postal codes. The purpose is usually to provide information that is only significant to people in a particular area, such as the scheduling of a meeting or the announcement of a public works project, but it can sometimes facilitate communication with groups that hold common issue or socioeconomic interests. Geographic targeting also facilitates personalized appeals such those displayed in the epigraph at the beginning of this chapter.

A more common form of targeting is to address mail to specific individuals. One way to do this is to obtain a list of people in particular groups such as veterans or senior citizens.[17] Another method is to keep a record of all those constituents who contact the office to register an opinion. Some members send out a survey asking constituents to indicate which issues they would like to receive information about. When the member wants to send mail to people with an interest in a particular issue, the staff simply looks in the database and knows every constituent who is known to be attentive to that subject matter.

Targeted mailings serve a very important strategic purpose by allowing members to speak exclusively to a specific audience. Just as a member can communicate a more specialized message when speaking to audiences at particular gatherings in his district, he can do the same through targeted mailings. The representative knows who he is speaking to and has a better idea about what they want to hear. This presents the opportunity to communicate different messages to various groups, or to send one message to an undifferentiated district audience and another to a specific group. Studying districtwide and targeted mail separately facilitates a good measurement of whether members are targeting audiences and what messages are being sent to each. This serves as a good approximation of the communication strategies utilized when appearing in front of various audiences in the district.

During interviews, staff members discussed the distinct strategic calculations behind the use of districtwide and targeted mail that can affect the types of messages sent in each. One senior staffer said, "Members will shade messages to targeted groups, but the messages can't stand in contrast to districtwide mail." He said that his office uses districtwide mailings as "educational tools" to make a pitch and lay out an argument on issues, while targeted mail is less educational and more promotional because "you already know the views of the recipients." Another staffer said that the representative he worked for sent different targeted mail messages to the portion of his district that was in the university community and to the part that was in the blue-collar area. Again, these were not contradictory statements, but ones that catered to the interests of each region. Targeted mail is sometimes used for specific political purposes. Staffers in one office said that they use targeted mail to "get the crossover vote," while another indicated that their purpose was to "charge up the base." These are all good examples of how targeted mail is used for specific strategic purposes just like speeches in the district made to particular groups.

Having discussed the basics of mass mailings and how they serve as a good proxy for all the messages sent by members to their constituents, in the next part I move on to explain the findings that resulted when I analyzed the content of this communication.

PART I CONTENT

3 MEMBERS' MESSAGES REGARDING CONGRESS

Were Congress able to demonstrate the political courage necessary to reduce and prioritize spending, this constitutional balanced budget amendment would not be necessary. However, the federal government has run a deficit for the last 24 years. Congress must stop mortgaging the future of our children and grandchildren, now!
—Letter sent by Marge Roukema (R-NY)
on 28 February 1994

I write this the morning after the House of Representatives completed action on the first 100 Days agenda, the Contract with America. This has been a remarkably productive legislative session. We have taken some giant steps forward in dealing with some of the problems challenging Americans of all ages.
—Newsletter sent by Roukema one year later (May 1995)

Before exploring the results of the analysis, I first examine what messages we may expect to find members communicating. I begin by analyzing what previous literature suggests about the incentives faced by members in regard to sending messages about congressional performance, then add to this the results of the surveys and interviews I conducted with members. These together form our expectations.

INCENTIVES SHAPING MEMBERS' MESSAGES ABOUT CONGRESSIONAL PERFORMANCE

Previous Research and Old Assumptions

Members of Congress are usually assumed to have three goals—reelection, good public policy, and power (both internal to the institution and external) (Fenno 1973). Since reelection is a necessary condition that must be met in order to facilitate the other two goals, it is usually considered the primary objective.[1] Members' goals are critical in shaping their strategic behavior, including communication. Therefore, predictions regarding the types of judgments of the institution that members send to their constituents should be based upon the assumption that they will engage in behavior that they presume aids their pursuit of these goals.

When Fenno observed members denigrating Congress while differentiating themselves from the institution, he explained their actions as rational behavior designed to help them win reelection. The positive aspect of this strategy is clear: if a member can convince her constituents that she is fighting for them against the institution, she can build trust. Trust is the objective of a member's home style because it helps her to achieve her primary goal of reelection. Fenno believed that "running against Congress" was "an appealing explanatory strategy because it is without cost" (168). That is, a member did not damage the chances of achieving any of her goals by sending this message. Although denigrating the institution was understood to have the potential of lowering constituents' approval of Congress, this result was not seen as having a negative impact on individual members.

There is, however, a potential electoral pitfall to this strategy. If a member of the public disapproves of the performance of the institution, he may also view his incumbent representative negatively. In this case encouraging constituents to view the institution unfavorably would be counterproductive to securing reelection. Fenno presumed that this strategy did not have a negative effect, though, because voters have bifurcated evaluation criteria for the institution and individual members. That is, for the individual members the "standard is one of representativeness—of personal style and policy views," while for the institution "standards emphasize efforts to solve national problems" (1975, 278). If the evaluation criteria were completely unlinked, members would not have to be concerned about how their constituents view Congress. Studies by Cook (1979) and Parker and Davidson (1979) supported the accuracy of the bifurcation presumption in the 1970s. They could not find any empirical evidence indicating that respondents' ratings of the institution affected evaluations of their representative.

While Fenno concentrated his explanation on the electoral benefits of this strategy, he did not address the potential impact that it could have on members' secondary goals. It is instructive to consider the incentives that these other goals may have produced at the time of Fenno's observations in the 1970s. The direct impact of this behavior on the goal of gaining power within the institution is usually minimal. Achieving power requires winning the favor of colleagues, usually fellow partisans, who will then grant formal or informal authority in the future. Most communication sent by a representative to his constituents is not heard by his colleagues and therefore has no effect on his reputation. This was especially true prior to 1979 when C-SPAN made the House floor a much more important forum for communicating with the public (the difference C-SPAN may have made toward this incentive is discussed later in this chapter). Even when representatives are aware of actions by their colleagues, the common practice is not to interfere with each other's activities aimed at constituents. Even when a member casts a vote on the floor against his party it is not unusual for a party leader to accept the simple explanation, "it's for the district."[2] This demonstrates the extent to which everyone needs to accept that reelection is every member's primary goal. Since replacement of members is usually a zero-sum game with partisan trade-offs (except in the rare cases of primary challenges), reelection is not only in the interest of individuals but also their parties.

Presuming that "running against Congress" could cause public approval of the institution to decline, this strategy could have an effect on members achieving their goal of creating good public policy. This would be a detrimental effect if low approval made it more difficult for members to cast the politically painful votes that are often necessary for the passage of significant legislation. Individual members find it essential to have the trust of their constituents so that they will be given the leeway to act in ways that are potentially controversial, such as when casting difficult votes. The same can be true for Congress as a whole. Just as representatives who have not developed trust are watched more closely and with more skepticism by their constituents, if the institution is seen as untrustworthy its actions will be viewed in a similar fashion by the public. This type of scrutiny can make it much more difficult for Congress to pass potentially controversial legislation. When voting, a member has to weigh his perceived value of the legislation along with the way his constituents are likely to view his vote. If Congress is distrusted it is much more likely that any legislation will be looked on less favorably by the public, thus making it more difficult for legislators to vote for it. If a member desires it to be easier for Congress to pass legislation he will want the institution to be looked upon more favorably.

The implications of the supposition that members desire good public policy must be more closely examined. It is not correct to equate the policy goal with wanting to make it easier for Congress to pass legislation. Some members, especially those in the minority, may feel that good policy will not be passed by the present Congress so they would prefer policy-making to be difficult. Even some members of the majority party may not want to make policy-making easier if they are ideologically opposed to what the congressional majority is likely to pass. Certainly this was the case for many Southern Democrats when it came to civil rights legislation in the 1960s. The argument made by congressional party government adherents such as Rohde (1991) is that the more liberal members of the Democratic majority changed the internal rules in the early 1970s to make it more difficult for the conservative party members to block new policies. If public attitudes toward the institution could also be used to make the passage of new policies more difficult, some members might want to do this in order to increase the probability of what they see as good public policy—the status quo.

Therefore we would assume that many members, especially those in the majority who are closely aligned ideologically with their party, would prefer for Congress to be trusted by the American public so that legislation being considered will not be viewed suspiciously. I also presume that members will not want to destroy permanently the reputation of the institution, or even for a limited time make Congress completely unable to operate. There is little purpose in being a member of an institution that cannot perform its primary function. In addition, there is the psychological desire to want any institution that one is so closely connected with to be viewed favorably by the public.

Those members who place a significant value on the institution's reputation will have an incentive to send positive judgments or at least refrain from sending negative messages about Congress. Although this is a very difficult factor to quantify, the level of a member's preference for institutional maintenance may be an important factor in predicting his behavior. However, the reality is that each individual member recognizes he probably can gain more toward his primary goal (reelection) by bashing Congress than he can gain toward any other goal by praising that institution. As long as a member feels the need to build trust with constituents to help his reelection goal, he may have an incentive to run against Congress. Fenno's findings about members' behavior appeared to confirm that this was indeed what representatives do when they communicate with their constituents.

Contemporary Incentives

Of course, Fenno's findings were based on limited observations of eighteen members made more than twenty-five years ago. The social scientific desire to seek validation of any study of behavior, especially one with such a small number of cases, may be reason enough to conduct another analysis of members' messages. But the passage of time makes a reexamination even more important when we consider the changes that have occurred in the congressional environment. As Fenno explains:

> All representatives are context interpreters. They will make choices and take actions not in the abstract, but according to what they believe to be rational and/or appropriate in the circumstances or context in which they find themselves. (2000, 6)

While I assume that members' goals have stayed the same, there are many reasons to believe that the context within which they are pursuing them has changed significantly. This means that different strategies may be appropriate, including those involving the communication of messages about congressional performance.

There have been notable findings concerning public attitudes toward Congress and its members, along with important new theories regarding congressional parties that suggest that some members may face incentives that do not encourage negativity toward the institution. Scholars have challenged the belief that voters have separate evaluation criteria for individual members and the institution. This assumption is critical to the "running against Congress" strategy. If a member thinks that his constituents' views of him are directly affected by their evaluations of the institution, he may not want to risk lowering public approval of congressional performance but would instead support Congress in his rhetoric.

Analysis of survey data has turned up evidence that there is a link between institutional and individual evaluations. Born found that "judgments of Congress's performance indeed served as strong predictors of members' reputations from 1978 to 1986" (1990, 223). In a similar study, Mangum (1996) examined the American National Election Study (ANES) and found that in 1988, 1990, and 1992 the popularity of representatives was affected by respondents' support for the institution. These findings suggest that the "running against Congress" strategy that Fenno labeled "costless" actually may prove very costly to individual members. If a member depresses the popularity of Congress among his constituents by denigrating the institution, he may be hurting his reelection chances. For this reason, he has an incentive to be positive toward the institution in an attempt to raise his constituents' evaluations of Congress. However, previous research has provided no evidence regarding how many members may hold this view of their incentives.

There is another electoral explanation for why we would not expect to see all members of Congress being negative toward the institution. This has to do with members seeing their reelection chances tied not to the popularity of the institution but to their party. The various congressional party theorists have produced some of the most contentious literature regarding Congress since the early 1990s.[3] The general thesis is that members of the majority party have electoral and/or policy incentives to empower their leaders to pursue a partisan legislative agenda; some theorists emphasize the policy incentives and others the electoral incentives. It is assumed that if the leadership can maintain the party discipline necessary to pass legislation favored by most of its members, it will not only serve policy goals but also build the party's reputation, hence increasing the electoral prospects of its members. This is because achieving the passage of good legislation will burnish the party's record among the public. Cox and McCubbins (1993) lay out the argument that a "party's record"—defined as "a commonly accepted summary of the past actions, beliefs, and outcomes with which it is associated" (110–11)—influences the election probabilities of its members. Therefore representatives have an electoral incentive to cultivate a good reputation for their party.

As explained by Rohde (1991), the ability and incentive for members to grant more powers to their leaders to encourage members to work together have grown since the 1970s. For many members, the increased ideological homogeneity of party membership in the electorate created an electoral incentive to support their party and facilitated the leadership's ability to promote a partisan agenda (170). This homogeneity means that a member doesn't have to "choose between keeping his party label at home and strengthening his party connections in Congress" (Fenno 1998, 77). When a member represents partisans who have views similar to those held by party leaders and most of his colleagues, all of his incentives are aligned, and he is very likely to engage in behavior that advances the party's legislative agenda.

With party leadership strengthened by members who shape the congressional agenda and promote the passage of the majority's preferred policies, the party's record becomes more closely connected with the reputation of the institution. This gives majority party members an electoral incentive not only to work internally for the party agenda but also to promote externally their party's reputation for successfully running the institution and creating good policy. But positive public opinion does not come from activities alone; it depends on perceptions that can be shaped through communication. Thus members of the majority party have an incentive not only to give powers to their leaders to promote the party agenda but also to contribute to the communication of positive messages about the party's performance. This is an important prediction that party government theories suggest in regard to the types of messages we would expect to see representatives communicating. But it has not been proponents of these theories that have made this argument explicitly, it has been a key detractor. Keith Krehbiel, who has disputed the claims that parties have a significant policy impact in Congress, has said that an "arguably necessary condition . . . in the partisan electoral-connection argument" is that "reelection seekers use their party labels and partisan voting records from the lawmaking arena when they compete in the electoral arena" (1998, 220). This expectation logically follows from party government theories, especially the one proposed by Cox and McCubbins.

Because members of Congress must be reelected every two years—in fact, some members face a primary election fourteen months after they start their term—they are often said to engage in a permanent campaign. That is, not only do they undertake strategic behavior in the months prior to an election, but they campaign for reelection throughout their terms. Therefore we should see members running with their parties all of the time. This should apply to members of both the majority and minority parties. While congressional party government adherents are mainly concerned with the majority party because the minority does not have many formal powers in the House, members of the minority do have the ability to communicate. Even if the minority cannot build its own record of legislative achievement in the House, its members can "run against Congress" and the majority party's control of the institution as they seek reelection under their party banner.

While party government theories explain a member's potential electoral and policy incentives for supporting her party, she may also have a further inducement based on her power goal. Although it most likely was not the case in the 1970s, a member's goal of gaining power inside Congress could also be promoted by sending either positive or negative messages about congressional performance. One way to gain power within the party is to participate in activities that the leadership views as helpful in achieving partisan goals. When leaders determine that it is advantageous to have members participate in communicating the party message, it may be in the interest of power-seeking representatives to lend their support. Of course, party leaders allow individual members to choose the messages that are best suited to winning the trust of constituents in their home districts.

Prior to the 1980s there were few opportunities for members to communicate to the public outside of their districts and hence not many chances to gain favor with leaders for helping with party communication. This situation has changed dramatically, most importantly with the introduction of C-SPAN in 1979. The House floor has always been a good place for sending messages to the public. There are a number of tailor-made message opportunities outside of legislative business including "one minutes," "morning hour," and "special orders."[4] However, before C-SPAN brought cameras into the House, all members could do to publicize their speeches on the floor was to send out printed copies. Today, activities on the floor are broadcast live to viewers via cable television with the possibility of later replay. This not only provides a much better opportunity for representatives to communicate their own messages to the public, but it has given parties another avenue for spreading their rhetoric. There has been a concerted effort, beginning especially in the 1990s, for party leaders to organize their members to take full advantage of every opportunity to broadcast strategic party messages (see Lipinski 2001b). Those representatives who want to advance in power in the House are much more likely to expend the time and effort to participate in these party-led activities. It is important to note that messages sent from the floor may be even more visible to constituents than votes cast. Only if a member chooses to "run with his party" for reelection will he communicate party messages from the floor.

Evidence Regarding Members' Partisan Incentives

The belief that members of the majority have an incentive to run with their parties and not against Congress is based on parties providing electoral, policy, and power incentives to engage in this behavior. It is important to consider the evidence we have to support this. As discussed earlier, some studies have indicated that voters' evaluations of their representatives are affected by their approval of Congress. If this were a nondifferentiated effect on all members then we might expect some representatives to "run with Congress" because of the electoral incentive, but there would be no partisan variation. However, the party strategy discussed earlier suggests that the public rewards and punishes only majority party members according to whether they have a favorable or unfavorable view of the institution. Recent studies suggest that voters do differentiate between incumbents of the majority and minority when voting based on congressional approval. Examining ANES surveys, Boucher and Cover (1996) found that individuals' evaluations of Congress appeared to affect vote choice in 1988, 1992, and 1994, but only if there was no control for the incumbent's partisan affiliation. They claim that "when the incumbent's partisan affiliation is included in the model of congressional vote choice, the anti-incumbent mood appears to in fact be anti-Democratic in nature" (1). That is, the antipathy of the public toward the institution only affected members of the majority party.

Hibbing and Tiritilli (2000) found even stronger evidence that voters increasingly reward and punish members of the majority according to their opinions of the institution. They claim that the public's willingness to attribute responsibility for the problems of Congress to the majority party and then to vote on this attribution was significant in the 1990s, much more so than in the 1970s. They demonstrate this by comparing the voting behavior of those who approve and disapprove of Congress. While over the past two decades voters who approved of Congress have always been more likely to vote for the majority party than those who disapproved, this gap in partisan vote choice was substantially larger in the 1990s. Both of these studies indicate that there are electoral incentives for members of both parties to "run with their parties" by either promoting or bashing Congress.

Party leaders put tremendous amounts of effort into encouraging their members to communicate partisan messages to the public (see Lipinski 2001b and chap. 4, this vol.). The partisan rhetoric that was promoted by some party leaders has notably included messages specifically about congressional performance. In the late 1980s and especially the early 1990s there was a concerted effort by some Republicans, led by Newt Gingrich (GA), to attack the institution in hopes that it would lead to the downfall of the Democrats who were in their third decade as House majority. Balz and Brownstein (1996) assert that Gingrich "incessantly portrayed the House as an institution corrupted by decades of entrenched power as part of his strategy to undermine public support for Democratic rule" (116). By consistently attacking Congress, the Republicans hoped to convince the public to vote to take control away from the Democrats. They were "confident that the fallout would harm Democrats much more than themselves" (27).

Republican members had incentives to buy into this strategy for the purposes of getting reelected, gaining partisan control of the House (which is advantageous for policy and power), and gaining favor with Gingrich who was clearly the ascendant leader. Gingrich first came to prominence in 1989 when he defeated Edward R. Madigan (IL) to become Republican whip. This triumph was a victory for the more conservative branch of the party and also a signal that the more aggressive, conflictual strategy promoted by the brash Georgian was being embraced by the Republicans. Reports on the election suggested that Republicans chose "Gingrich's knack for strategy and putting out a clear partisan message, which many see as necessary to winning political campaigns," over "Madigan's skill at building coalitions needed to influence legislation passed in a Democratic-dominated House" (Hook 1989a, 565). The minority leader, Robert H. Michel, said that the election told the leadership that the rank and file "want us to be more activated and more visible and more aggressive" (Hook 1989b, 625).

All of this points to Republican members having clear incentives created by their party and its leaders to "run against Congress" in an attempt to change their minority status. In doing so minority party members are seeking to diminish the reputation of the majority party. The minority party has little hope of being able to build a positive party record through legislative accomplishments because House rules grant consequential procedural powers to the majority. The minority party thus has to rely on message-sending not connected to the passage of legislation, combined with attacks on the record of the majority party. When the minority party tries to build its own record through communication unconnected to the legislative process it is unlikely that its message will be widely heard and have much of an impact on the public. This was seen in 1994 when Republicans used the Contract with America to try to nationalize the election. Despite the efforts made to publicize this list of policies that the party would work to implement if elected to the majority, a CBS/*New York Times* preelection poll (3 November 1994) revealed that 71 percent of voters had never heard of the Contract. The difficulty that a congressional minority party has informing the American public about a proposed positive agenda makes it much more attractive to rely on attacking the majority's record.

Republican efforts to attack Congress demonstrate what an important strategy this can be for the minority in order to undermine public support for the majority party's control of the institution. In such communication "Congress" becomes a proxy for the majority party, and messages evaluating institutional performance are really suggestions about how well the majority is running the institution. But this is not likely to be a debate engaged in only by one party. If the minority can gain an advantage by attacking Congress, the majority would logically progress by promoting the institution. To do this, members of the majority will send the message that Congress is performing well and they are responsible for this. In other words, members of the majority have an incentive to promote the institution and "run *with* Congress."

Members' Views of Their Incentives

The next step in developing expectations about members' behavior is to move beyond what has been observed and examine what representatives see as their incentives to communicate strategic messages about Congress. After all, even if outside observations of the context are accurate, representatives may have different views. In order to measure members' attitudes I look at the responses given to the survey I conducted.

If members are attempting to send judgments of the institution as proxies for the majority party's record, they must believe that their constituents will see actions attributed to "Congress" as the deeds of the majority party. Members were asked whether when they were communicating they ever used the terms *Congress* or *House* and intended their constituents to understand this as meaning the majority party. This practice was admitted to by 42 percent of the representatives—or about half of the 86 percent who said that they have ever sent judgments of Congress to constituents. This is a high number to admit engaging in this practice, especially in light of the fact that this breaks at least the spirit of the franking rules. In general, the rules of the House say that references to parties are supposed to be limited to situations in which they are directly relevant to the legislative process and are not to be used for political advantage. An even more convincing 89 percent of representatives believe that "other members" purposely use institutional terms as substitutes for naming the majority party when sending messages of praise or criticism. Thus it is clear that when we examine the content of mass mailings we must understand that mentions of the institution are often meant to be references to the majority.

I also asked members about the effect that they believe low congressional approval has on an incumbent's reelection probability. These results show whether members presume voters' evaluation criteria for the institution and individual representatives are linked or separate. Only 25 percent of representatives suggested a belief in bifurcated evaluation criteria by responding that low congressional approval does not affect the vote for an incumbent of either party. These members would not engage in rhetoric about congressional performance based on partisan incentives. They could potentially utilize the "running against Congress" tactic suggested by Fenno since their interpretation fits a key presumption underlying this strategy. However, the other three-fourths of representatives did not hold this view. More than two-thirds agreed that when a voter disapproves of Congress she is less likely to vote for an incumbent member of the majority party. Incumbents in the majority who hold this belief would have an incentive to try to improve their constituents' views of Congress if they presumed they could.

There is a split in members' opinions concerning the effect of disapproval on those in the minority. Forty percent believe that disapproval of Congress makes a constituent *less* likely to vote for an incumbent minority party member, while 21 percent assume that it makes a person *more* likely to vote for their representative. This suggests that some legislators think it can be electorally helpful to party members to try to lower public opinion of the institution, while others have the opposite view. It is important to note that survey respondents were overwhelmingly Democrats who had recently survived the devastating 1994 elections. These members were likely very conscious of the impact that low approval of Congress had on many Democrats, but they may not have been willing to link the impact only to members of the Democratic majority.

The most important point that the survey results demonstrate is that members' beliefs differ in regard to the electoral impact of their constituents' views of the institution. It is crucial to recognize that not all representatives will look at the same circumstances and see identical strategic possibilities. One reason for this is that politicians are never sure exactly what actions have worked for them in the past, but they tend to follow strategies that have seemed to be helpful. These won't be the same for everyone. As Jacobson has said, "Successful candidates are inclined to do what they did in the past; they must have done something right, even if they cannot be sure what; a degree of superstition is understandable" (2001, 82). While it's still possible to generalize about members' behavior, our expectations about the behavior of individuals must allow for some degree of variance no matter how much we know about external circumstances.

The survey responses show that almost two-thirds of the members (64 percent) believe that low public approval of Congress makes it more difficult to pass significant legislation. In replying to an open-response survey question, respondents explained how members' reactions to low approval hurt policy-making. The attitude of many representatives can be summed up by the member who said that when public approval is low, "fear of negative publicity causes some members of Congress to not want to make waves and therefore they shy away from significant legislation, which by definition, would inspire significant opposition." The belief that public attitudes can cause members to be fearful was echoed by another representative who stated, "Members tend to fear public opinion if Congress is despised." When low public approval causes fear it "makes members too unwilling to take political risks on issues." As similarly stated by another member, "The more popular Congress, the easier it is for members to cast correct but politically difficult votes." When members cannot cast difficult votes it is not easy to address complex issues.

What members fear is the possibility of losing the support of some constituents if they champion the wrong side of a controversial issue. There are a number of sources that could serve to rally public ire against an individual incumbent. One source is other members who utilize public disapproval to mobilize opposition to policies with which they disagree. As one representative stated, "To all policy objections . . . cynical objections can be added, impugning the motives of those advancing the legislation." That is, those members who disagree with a policy can find a way to attach public cynicism to that particular proposal. When a policy option is viewed negatively by the public, those members who support it will likely lose some of the trust of constituents.

Even if no one is utilizing public ire to their own advantage, a few representatives complained that when the public has a low opinion of Congress they often become more apathetic about the process. Public apathy itself makes policy-making more difficult. One member stated: "If the public has a low opinion of Congress they are less likely to become engaged in the political process. Public opinion is crucial to moving legislation. When the public is disengaged, that becomes more difficult." Other problems arise because general public apathy means "lobbyists have more influence." Another representative claimed that when public approval is low, "interest groups have more success in public campaigns on their issues." Thus low public approval of Congress is seen as detrimental to policy-making because it can raise the potential for demagoguery, it can enable lobbyists and interest groups to have greater influence on the process, and it can simply cause a lack of the momentum necessary for passage of any major legislation. Members who want policy-making to be easier will desire stronger public support for Congress, while those who want more roadblocks will prefer disapproval of the institution.

Expectations

What we have seen thus far suggests that there will be members who send messages about the institution driven by their partisanship. The survey responses show that when communicating with constituents, representatives will use "Congress" as a proxy for the majority party controlling the institution. Therefore I expect that not all members will run against Congress, but we will see variation among representatives in the messages they send about institutional performance. We must also consider that while the ideological diversity inside the two parties has narrowed, there is still variance among partisans. The farther away a representative is from the mainstream of her party, the less likely she is to be influenced by partisan incentives. This leads me to expect variance in members' positive and negative judgments of the institution, with partisanship being the most important—but not the only—factor explaining the differences. As the survey responses demonstrate, members differ in how they view their incentives for being positive or negative. Some representatives believe that voters' evaluation criteria for the institution and individuals are bifurcated, meaning that "running against Congress"—as an institution, not just as a party proxy—may be seen as a valuable strategy.

As noted earlier, we do not have evidence corroborating Fenno's findings. Neither do we have any indication that members are actually sending the types of messages suggested by party government theories and running with their parties when seeking election. The only evidence we have has been offered by Krehbiel (1998). He does not look directly at members' comments about congressional performance, but instead examines campaign ads to find whether members are referring favorably to their parties. Citing anecdotes from a few congressional campaigns in 1994 and 1996, Krehbiel reaches the conclusion that "the party label seems more like a bad-luck charm than a treasured brand name" (223). This indicates that representatives are not promoting their parties in their campaign rhetoric as party government theories suggest we would find. If this is the case we should not expect to see members of the majority "running with Congress" when we analyze their messages sent to constituents. Since this is the only evidence we have to go on so far, it is imperative that we conduct a much more thorough investigation to see whether Krehbiel's admittedly "qualitative and somewhat soft" evidence (220) can be corroborated or the expectations cited earlier are correct.

WHAT MESSAGES ABOUT CONGRESS LOOK LIKE

Policies

There are two distinct facets of congressional performance about which members send judgments to their constituents—policy choices (or, more explicitly, the purported impact of these policy choices) and congressional processes (that is, how Congress operates). The importance of representatives' appraisals of the impact of policy choices is clear.

Since the primary job of Congress is to pass legislation, the public will make assessments about how the institution is performing based to some extent on their impressions of whether the policies passed (or not passed) are good or bad. Whenever a member discusses the impact of policies acted upon by Congress—be it in the form of policies approved, rejected, or in some other way addressed—he directly or indirectly expresses an opinion about the institution's performance.

A member can take a stance on policy content either in regard to a specific piece of legislation or a set of policy actions. The excerpt from Marge Roukema's (R-NY) 1995 newsletter at the beginning of this chapter is a good example of a member praising a general pattern of policy actions by Congress. She claims, "We [members of Congress] have taken some giant steps forward in dealing with some of the problems challenging Americans of all ages." No issues are singled out, but Roukema is unquestionably judging Congress positively. In the same way, representatives will criticize Congress for a general failure to address problems. In his 1992 newsletter, Bill Zeliff (R-NH) complains, "Most frustrating to members of Congress with business backgrounds is the failure of Congress to deal with many major issues facing America."

More often members send constituents assessments of Congress based on legislative action regarding specific issues. Oftentimes Congress is praised or criticized for legislation that impacts the general public. A newsletter sent by Ed Towns (D-NY) to all his constituents in the summer of 1994 contained praise for Congress for passage of legislation with nonparticularized benefits.

> In spite of the long winter of 1994, Congress maintained a steady legislative pace. We were able to enact the Federal Workforce Restructuring Act which will save the federal government $35 billion over the next five years. In addition, we passed a comprehensive anti-crime bill which maintains a balance between enforcement and prevention.

Saving money and preventing crime are public goods. But more often Congress was the target of criticism for its spending habits and the federal budget deficit. In a 1992 districtwide newsletter Bill Zeliff (R-NH) complained, "If you give Congress more money, it will spend all of that money and then some!"

Some issues are of interest to particular groups. One of the groups most often targeted in mass mailings is veterans. In a newsletter sent to veterans in 1991, Jack Fields (R-TX) gives a positive judgment of congressional policies in an article entitled "New Benefits Package Passed by Congress." Fields bestows praise by saying, "Congress has approved

... legislation designed to benefit those troops who served in operations Desert Shield and Desert Storm." While targeted messages often give credit for provision of a particularized benefit, sometimes Congress is portrayed as a villain. A negative judgment of Congress for taking action affecting a particular group can be seen in Gerald Kleczka's (D-WI) Year-End Report newsletter. He asserts:

> Congress recently approved legislation ... to allow corporations to raid worker pension plans. Earlier this year, the House passed a bill which would permit companies to withdraw the excess in worker pension plans and use it for any purpose.

Kleczka's sharp criticism of Congress comes in reference to legislation that he claims will hurt workers who are counting on these pension benefits.

A final category of issues on which members judge congressional policies are those of interest specifically to district residents. This category includes mostly positive statements regarding public works projects approved for the district. Members sometimes give credit only to themselves when discussing these types of benefits. In situations such as this, the member is not considered to have sent a message about the institution. A good example of Congress being given credit for district benefits is in Jerry Costello's (D-IL) 1993 "Year-End Report to Constituents."

> Congress passed a $6 billion flood package in August ...
> Congress appropriated $3 million for a new Clean Coal Technology Center ...
> Congress approved $7.8 million to complete construction on the Price Lock & Dam ...
> Congress appropriated $10 million at my request for relocation of Cardinal Village at Scott [AFB] ...

There were, however, a few instances in which members criticized Congress for actions that were claimed to be harmful to the district. A letter sent by Ed Towns (D-NY) announcing a town hall meeting in April 1995 claims:

> The House of Representatives has recently passed new initiatives which will greatly reduce Federal programs which are currently coming into New York City.

Representative Towns does not specifically mention his district but his constituents know that the programs that have been targeted are important to them as residents of New York City.

Processes

The impact of individuals' views of processes on their opinions about government has been thoroughly explicated by John Hibbing and Elizabeth Theiss-Morse (1995, 2002). In *Congress as Public Enemy* they argue that "dissatisfaction with political institutions and especially Congress is due in no small part to public perceptions of the processes involved" (1995, 1). While not dismissing the effect of policy content on congressional approval, Hibbing and Theiss-Morse emphasize the importance of the way the public views "how . . . policy was arrived at" (1995, 14). They claim that "public concerns with process come down to two components: procedural efficiency (making decisions in an expeditious and direct manner) and procedural equity (access, attention, and benefits being allocated in an equitable and just manner)" (1995, 14). In the follow-up book, *Stealth Democracy* (2002), they simplify their argument by saying that "judgments influenced by process can be made by anyone who has an opinion of whether politicians are self-serving or not" (237–38).

Comments made regarding processes are qualitatively different from those concerning policies. Praising or attacking the degree to which the process is efficient and equitable exalts or impugns the competency and intentions of those who run the institution, especially the leadership. A tainted process suggests that citizens should not expect Congress to be productive in producing fair policies. Since the majority party has significant control over the policy-making process in the House, these messages are often more blatantly partisan than comments about policies, which can cut across party lines.

When I looked for process statements in mailings I used a definition that is based to some extent on the ideas from the first book by Hibbing and Theiss-Morse (1995). Messages about congressional processes can be placed into two categories. The first involves comments that directly concern the rules by which the legislative process is conducted. These statements can take the form of attacks on the leadership for unfairly manipulating the legislative agenda or other criticism of the regulations used to govern policy-making. Such statements are references to the efficiency and equity of the process. The second category concerns comments that refer to whether the individuals who create policies—that is, other members—can be trusted to make good decisions or are a part of a corrupt system. If the public believes that members are not responsible in their personal dealings with and management of the House Bank, the House dining room, or the post office, then they cannot trust members to make appropriate policy-making decisions. Hibbing and Theiss-Morse claim that the public believes that "members are quickly corrupted by special interests and lobbyists, by the office perquisites they receive, and by the people who surround and indulge them," and "the various congressional scandals that hit the media simply provide proof that public judgment is correct" (1995, 62).

My interviews with congressional staff members responsible for sending mailings suggest that there is a widespread belief that constituents have little interest in hearing about processes.[5] Many of the staffers I spoke with said that they generally do not mention it in their mailings because—in the words of one Hill veteran—"process is not relevant to people's lives, they want to know about outcomes." When constituents are viewed as exclusively results-oriented it does not make sense to waste resources and risk boring readers by writing about congressional processes in mailings. It doesn't pay to try to explain to them something they don't care to hear; as one staffer said, "you can get them to taste the pudding, but you can't get them to read the recipe." A few congressional staff members disagreed and said that their constituents *are* interested in the process. One replied that it is important to talk to constituents about how Congress is operating because "people take a lot of ownership in Washington and it working like it should." The lack of interest in sending messages about processes was reflected in survey responses that indicated only 27 percent of representatives admitted to having "praised or criticized internal activities of Congress" in their mailings.[6]

When examining messages about process in the mailings I found that the House majority leadership is often the target of attacks on the way the legislative process is run. In a summer 1994 newsletter, David Levy (R-NY) criticized the House leadership for not allowing a vote on legislation designed to cut spending.

> When the "A to Z" measure was introduced, 229 members of Congress cosponsored the bill. Opponents of the measure, including Democratic leaders who control the legislative agenda, have blocked efforts to hold hearings on the bill or bring it to a vote.

Republican leaders were also the subject of criticism when they took control of Congress in 1995. In November, Henry Waxman (D-CA) sent a newsletter claiming that "the new majority wouldn't allow a single hearing on its far-reaching Medicare proposal."

Other judgments of process refer directly to the rules that are in place to govern the operation of the institution. Dan Frisa (R-NY), in a 1995 newsletter, praised Congress for passing internal reforms.

> The <u>new</u> congress, with Republicans in control for the first time in forty years, has already brought about wholesale changes to Washington, D.C. Congressman Dan Frisa said "we've kept our promises; we've reformed Congress itself, and we've begun to re-make the entire federal government. It's about time!"
> - Congress now required to live under <u>all</u> laws . . .

Congress is also the subject of a fair amount of criticism for not responding to the American people in the legislative process. Joel Hefley (R-CO), in his winter 1992 newsletter, asserted:

> It's time Congress got off its high horse and listened to what the people of America want. Unless Congress shapes up, voter anger will continue to grow and the House of Representatives will lose all credibility as "The People's House."

Scandals involving the House Bank, the House dining room, and the post office were widely commented upon in the early 1990s. Republicans were especially anxious to use these to suggest that major changes were necessary in the House. In a letter dated 20 March 1992, David Dreier (R-CA) sent a thinly disguised call for ouster of the Democratic majority.

> The House Bank, restaurant, and post office scandals are clear indications that this institution should be under new management. Some of us have called for an independent investigation so that we can begin to address the high priority items that the American people want us to resolve.

While most comments about scandals were attacks on members' behavior, some messages were sent attempting to explain that these actions were not as bad as they appeared. Major Owens (D-NY) sent a letter in November 1991 defending Congress and attacking the media for diverting attention from real problems.

> In recent months, the media has had a field day attacking Congress for its perceived misuse of your hard-earned tax dollars. You have

undoubtedly seen a great deal in the press about Congressmembers bouncing checks in the House of Representatives' bank and in its restaurant, among other such stories. What the media did not say is that taxpayers' money was not at all involved in these situations. In fact, the stories served no other purpose than to divert your attention from the real bandits of this nation—the corporate bandits . . .

This was a tactic utilized by a number of members. The motivation for these messages, however, was likely not just defending Congress. The representatives who sent messages such as this in 1992 all had a large number of bank overdrafts.

Gridlock

There is a type of judgment that overlaps both policy and process categories—criticisms of legislative gridlock or praise for the institution being especially productive in passing legislation. These messages were counted in both categories. When a representative sends such a message he is saying not only that good policies are (or are not) being passed, but also that congressional processes are (or are not) working effectively to facilitate fair and efficient policy-making. An example of such a judgment is the claim "The House of Representatives made significant progress this year in breaking the deadlock that has gripped Capitol Hill." A "deadlock" implies processes are not working as they are supposed to, and the suggestion is that good policies are not being passed. Therefore this claim is considered to be a positive judgment about both policies and processes.[7]

In the early 1990s, members often talked about gridlock and the inability of Congress to "get anything done." One example appears in a newsletter sent by Jim Bacchus (D-FL) in 1992.

> Today, in the wake of various scandals and government gridlock, the need for fundamental change is clear. We must move quickly toward long overdue reforms—not only to end unwarranted privileges, but also to make our government more responsive to the challenges our country faces today.

In 1993 many Democrats proclaimed that the process was fixed when they gained unified control of the government and were able to "break gridlock." Earl Hilliard (D-AL) in a 1994 districtwide newsletter proclaimed, "We broke the political gridlock in Congress for the first time in over twelve years by passing the Budget Act." In 1995 the Republicans made this same claim after they took over Congress for the first time in forty years and passed a number of pieces of legislation promised in their Contract with America. The preceding excerpt from Dan Frisa's 1995 newsletter is a typical example of Republicans' claims about breaking gridlock in the 104th Congress.

AGGREGATE RESULTS

Frequency of Members Sending Messages about Congressional Performance

In order to examine members' messages I developed a content code that systematically measured the positive and negative comments about congressional performance contained in all the mailings sent in the 100 districts in my sample (see appendix B for the complete code).[8] Table 1 shows the percentage of members in each year who sent any messages about congressional performance in at least one mailing during a session. On average, almost three out of four representatives sent such messages each year, and this did not vary appreciably from year to year. The years that saw the highest percentages of representatives sending these types of messages were 1992 and 1995. It is not surprising that 1995 produced so many comments since the Republicans had just taken control of the House for the first time in forty years and passed myriad new and sometimes controversial pieces of legislation.

There are a number of reasons there were so many judgments of Congress sent in 1992. This was the year in which numerous congressional scandals came to light and were focused upon by the news media. Many members addressed these revelations in order to make political

TABLE 1. Members Who Sent Any Messages about Congressional Performance (in percentages)

	1991	1992	1993	1994	1995	Average
Any	71 (100)	78 (99)	67 (100)	66 (100)	76 (100)	72 (499)
Republicans	77 (35)	83 (35)	68 (34)	59 (34)	71 (49)	72 (187)
Democrats	68 (65)	75 (64)	67 (66)	70 (66)	80 (51)	71 (312)
Policies	69	77	64	65	75	70
Republicans	74	77	59	56	69	67
Democrats	66	76	67	70	80	71
Process	13	30	18	19	25	21
Republicans	26	54	23	21	26	30
Democrats	6	19	15	18	23	16

Note: N given in parentheses.

points or minimize damage. This was also a presidential election year, and especially in a time of divided government there was a significant amount of battling going on between the parties as each tried to send messages that might aid its presidential candidate. Public anxiety about the state of the national economy and the budget deficit likely induced members to try to demonstrate that they were responding to these crises. One other critical factor engendering more judgments in 1992 was the occurrence of the first election in the new districts created in the decennial remapping. Redistricting meant that many members needed to send messages introducing themselves to new constituents.

The percentage of members sending messages regarding policy choices far exceeded the number sending comments about processes in each session, with 70 percent on average commenting on policies and 21 percent on processes. The relatively low percentage of representatives commenting on processes fits with the prevailing viewpoint I found in my interviews with congressional staffers. The year in which the most members sent these judgments was 1992. This was the year that produced a number of embarrassing revelations about the actions of individual members and the way in which congressional rules allowed such activities. These included the overdrafts at the House Bank, unpaid meal bills at the House restaurant, and problems at the internal post office. All of these incidents fed the public image of members of Congress being out of touch with the people they were supposed to be representing and suggested that something was wrong with the way Congress was being run. In addition, Ross Perot's presidential campaign in 1992 made Americans more conscious of the way the government was operating.

In the 103d Congress the number of members sending process judgments was lower and the topics of these judgments changed. Since the Democrats now had unified control of both Congress and the presidency they were sending messages about the end of gridlock, praising Congress for being free from the paralysis in the policy-making process that had been preventing the enactment of important legislation. At the same time, Republicans were continuing to attack the way that the Democratic leadership was conducting the business of the institution. In 1995—after the Republicans captured the House for the first time in forty years—there was an increase in the number of members sending process judgments, although it did not reach the 1992 level. Republicans were hailing changes in the House's internal policies and procedures, while some Democrats were criticizing the way that the new House leadership was running the institution.

It is important to note that over 90 percent of the members who made a comment about processes also sent judgments of policy. That is to say that comments about processes were mostly made in addition to ones about policy content. On average, Republicans were almost twice as likely as Democrats to send judgments about processes, suggesting that there was a difference in strategies between members of the two parties.

Frequency of Members Sending Positive and Negative Messages

Next I examine the extent to which members made positive and negative evaluations of Congress. A member was considered to have been positive in a congressional session if he sent at least twice as many positive pieces of mail as negative pieces during the year. Representatives were categorized as negative using analogous criteria. If a member sent both positive and negative judgments in a session, but neither outweighed the other by a two-to-one margin, he was placed in the mixed category.

The results revealed in table 2 indicate that members clearly are not all "running against Congress." Instead, there is an almost three-to-one margin of representatives who are positive to those who are negative. On average, almost 50 percent of the legislators sent predominantly positive messages about Congress to their constituents. In contrast, slightly less than one-fifth communicated predominantly negative comments. The number of representatives who sent mixed messages was very low (7 percent), indicating that most send highly consistent messages to their constituents. Since all members probably have a choice between discussing issues presenting Congress in a positive or a negative light, it is clearly a strategic decision for most to communicate only one type of message.

Examining members of each party separately exposes findings that appear somewhat consistent with the expectations of congressional party government theories. The results shown in table 3 suggest that membership in the majority or minority party is very important in pre-

TABLE 2. Members Sending Positive Messages, Negative Messages, No Messages, and Mixed Messages (in percentages)

	1991	1992	1993	1994	1995	Average
Positive	53	52	44	46	42	47
Negative	11	15	17	16	27	17
Mixed	7	11	6	4	7	7
None	29	22	33	34	24	28

dicting whether a representative will be positive or negative. It is apparent that majority party members (Democrats from 1991 to 1994, and Republicans in 1995) are more likely than those in the minority to send positive messages and much less inclined to be negative. When control of the institution changed hands in 1995 for the first time in forty years, both Democrats and Republicans immediately shifted the messages they were sending. This clearly demonstrates that representatives in both parties use the institution as a proxy for the majority and communicate messages supporting their party.

The data in this table also indicate, however, that partisanship does not explain all the variance among members. There are other factors besides partisanship that affect the messages that members send about the institution. While negativity is largely (though not completely) explained by party membership (there are never more than 5 percent of majority party members sending these judgments), a significant number of minority party members in each session are positive. This suggests that some members of the minority find it strategically valuable to be positive.

The trend through the five years indicates an increasing polarization of the parties. While in 1991 the minority party was not overwhelmingly negative, in the next four years whichever party was in the minority was significantly more negative than positive toward Congress. When the Democrats lost control of Congress, they were even more likely to be negative than Republicans were in the previous year. The biggest change evident is the decrease in the number of minority party members sending positive judgments (see table 3): there was an approximately 50 percent drop in the number of Republicans sending positive messages from 1991 to 1992 and again from 1992 to 1993. Despite being in the minority, 37 percent of Republicans in 1991 and 17 percent in 1992 were positive in their communication about Congress. In fact,

TABLE 3. Members Sending Positive and Negative Messages by Party (in percentages)

	1991	1992	1993	1994	1995
Positive	53	52	44	46	42
Democrats	62	72	62	65	16
Republicans	37	17	9	9	69
Negative	11	15	17	16	27
Democrats	2	2	2	5	51
Republicans	29	40	47	38	2

in 1991 a higher percentage of Republicans communicated positive messages than sent negative ones.

The drop from 1991 to 1992 in the number of Republicans being positive likely resulted from changes in the political environment. In 1991 after the American victory in the Persian Gulf War, the Republican president was riding high in opinion polls and the mood of the nation was positive. Congressional response to the president's call to go to war provided Republican representatives with an issue to be positive about, and they also likely responded to the general public mood. In 1992, however, the public's disposition soured as the nation found itself in an economic recession. In addition, there was a very competitive presidential election with a strong third-party candidate (Ross Perot) reflecting the high level of discontent among the American public. These conditions gave Republican members little to praise Congress for and generally discouraged positive messages about the institution.

From 1992 to 1993 there was a further drop in the number of Republicans being positive. There are two explanations for this change in behavior among Republicans; one relates to the political environment and the other is a strategic choice. With the Republicans losing the White House they no longer controlled any branch of government that could be used to shape policy. This gave Republicans fewer policies that they could send positive messages about. Another very important cause was the deliberate change in tactics by House Republicans as the more confrontational wing of the party took charge of almost every leadership post in December 1992. The party was now being led by people like Newt Gingrich who believed that the best way to wrest power away from the Democrats was to relentlessly communicate negative messages about the institution (see also chap. 4, this vol.).

Although this change over time occurred in the number of Republicans being positive, table 4 shows that this was restricted to comments about policies. The number of Republicans who were positive about processes was extremely small throughout the four years of Democratic control. As discussed previously, Republicans were much more likely to send any messages about processes. These comments were overwhelmingly negative until their party took control. So the behavioral difference between the parties was not just that Republicans sent more messages about processes in the early period, but that these comments were always much more likely to be negative. This is probably because, as mentioned earlier, part of Newt Gingrich's strategy for capturing the House was to attack the way the Democrats were running the institution. As Ronald Elving explained in 1989, Gingrich had a strategy for taking down the Democrats beginning "with an attack on Democratic entrenchment and the institution's mores" (722). Democrats increased the number of comments they sent about processes but never matched the Republicans.

Table 4 also shows differences in the usage of comments about policies and processes. Not only are messages about policies much more prevalent, but the ratio of positive to negative comments in each are very different. Almost half of representatives sent positive messages about policies, while only 16 percent were negative. Members who sent comments about processes, however, were split evenly between those who were positive and those who were negative. This demonstrates the need to further examine the differences in the factors that motivate positive and negative messages regarding these two different facets of congressional performance (see chap. 4).

One other important aspect of communication is the difference in the use of targeted and districtwide mail. The use of mail sent districtwide to communicate messages about Congress declined in relation to the use of targeted mail. Overall, general mail was used to a greater extent to send messages about congressional performance, but as the use of this type of mail declined and targeted mail rose, both were utilized to an equal extent for this purpose in 1995. One obvious change that occurred in the use of targeted mail was the percentage of members who sent comments about Congress *only* in targeted mail. This was a reflection of the increasing tendency of members to send targeted mail instead of districtwide mail. It was a change that occurred because cuts

TABLE 4. Members Sending Positive and Negative Messages about Policies and Processes by Party (in percentages)

	1991	1992	1993	1994	1995	Average
Policies						
Positive	56	58	45	46	42	49
Republicans	46	29	9	9	69	35
Democrats	62	73	64	65	16	58
Negative	9	13	16	12	30	16
Republicans	20	34	41	26	0	22
Democrats	3	2	3	4	59	12
Processes						
Positive	3	10	9	11	18	10
Republicans	0	3	3	3	24	8
Democrats	5	14	12	15	12	11
Negative	10	21	8	8	6	11
Republicans	26	51	18	18	2	21
Democrats	1	5	3	3	10	4

in mail funds caused fewer pieces of mail to be sent, and advances in computer technology made targeted mailings easier.

As mentioned earlier, targeted mail serves an important role because it can be used to communicate specific messages to groups whose preferences are already known. In this way it is similar to making speeches in front of specialized gatherings in the district. When Fenno discusses members "running against Congress" in *Home Style,* much of what he refers to is speechmaking to specific groups. It is possible that members are communicating positive messages about congressional performance when they are sending messages aimed at all their constituents, but when they address more select groups they attack the institution. If representatives are engaging in this type of behavior we should see the differences in table 5. However, there is no clear discrepancy in the type of messages sent in targeted and districtwide mail. The average proportion of members who are positive to those who are negative is nearly identical in each. For every representative who is negative there are three being positive whether we look at messages sent to general or targeted audiences. In addition, further examination shows that in less than 1 percent of the cases did a representative send positive messages about Congress in districtwide mail and negative ones in targeted mail. Clearly most members are not being positive when speaking to all constituents and the negative when addressing specific groups.[9]

It is also important to examine whether representatives are using targeted mail to send positive messages to some audiences and negative messages to others. That is, are members being consistent in their evaluations of congressional performance, or do they simply try to tell the audience what they believe the listeners want to hear? If targeted mail was being used in the latter manner we should see a large number of

TABLE 5. Members Sending Positive and Negative Messages by Type of Mail (in percentages)

	1991	1992	1993	1994	1995	Average
Districtwide	53	68	44	44	50	52
Positive	36	44	32	36	28	35
Negative	9	18	9	7	17	12
Mixed	8	5	3	1	5	4
Targeted	42	43	39	47	50	44
(Targeted only)	(18)	(10)	(33)	(22)	(26)	(20)
Positive	35	33	23	31	30	30
Negative	4	4	12	14	17	10
Mixed	3	6	4	2	3	4

members who are categorized as sending mixed messages. However, we see that only 4 percent of representatives send mixed messages in targeted mail, the same small percentage that do this in mail sent districtwide. This indicates that when members are communicating with distinct groups of constituents they generally are not sending significantly different messages regarding the institution. Instead, these results suggest that representatives choose a message to send about Congress and follow through with this no matter who their audience is. We would expect to find members sending the same messages whether they are standing in front of a diverse crowd of constituents or a specific group. I will further examine the use of districtwide and targeted mail in the next chapter.

In this chapter I was able to show that, indeed, the conventional wisdom does not hold, and many members run with Congress. The cross-tabulations suggest that membership in the majority or minority party is significant in predicting who is positive and who is negative about congressional performance. This appears to support the implications of congressional party government theories in the electoral arena. But in order to confirm these findings it is essential to consider other factors that may have an impact on the messages members send. In the next chapter I build and test a multivariate model that facilitates further examination of the effects of partisanship and helps us to better understand the variation among members in their communication behavior.

4 RUNNING WITH THE PARTY

The 104th Congress has adopted in the House a series of proposals—cast as a "Contract with America"—that would reverse precious gains we have made to improve the quality of life and equity in our nation.
—Democrat Ron Dellums (CA) in spring/summer newsletter, 1995

For the first time in a long time the "new majority" in the House of Representatives demonstrated to the American people that we can deliver.
—Republican Robert Dornan (CA) in letter, August 1995

Having demonstrated that some members "run against Congress" by sending negative messages but more "run with Congress" by communicating positive messages, the next step is to explain the variance. While membership in the majority or minority party appears to be a strong predictor of these messages, it does not completely account for the differences. In order to better explain the variance among members I developed and tested a model of factors hypothesized to have an impact on the messages that members send.

THE MODEL

Instead of using a dichotomous variable gauging majority or minority party status, I employ a more complex variable that includes a measure of a member's level of party loyalty.[1] Members will probably vary in their likelihood of running with their party depending on how closely they choose to affiliate themselves with the party. A member's level of party support is usually measured by his party unity voting score.[2] This score reflects the percentage of party unity votes in a session—votes on which more than 50 percent of one party opposed more than 50 percent of the other party—on which the member supported his party. The more often a member votes with his party, the greater the probability that he will want to attach the party's reputation to himself. The more a member desires this attachment, the greater the likelihood that he will support the party in the messages he sends about the institution. Therefore, I include in the model a measure of the member's party unity score for the year. In order to place all members, no matter their party, on a common 100-point scale I constructed a Majority Support Score. This provides a measure of the level of support a representative gives to the majority party. For a member of the majority this is simply his party unity score, and for someone in the minority it is 100 minus his party unity score.[3] The higher a representative's score, the more likely he is to send positive messages about congressional performance.

A representative may make a decision to support his party based on his electoral strategy, his commitment to the party agenda, the desire to gain power, or some other reason. In order to provide a separate test of the impact of the reelection goal, I also included in the model a measure of the partisanship of district voters. It is assumed that communicating messages that constituents want to hear will help build trust and aid reelection. Therefore, representatives will react to their constituents' partisanship when determining whether to send positive or negative messages about Congress. The greater the number of voters in a district who support the party that controls the House, the more likely a representative will be to send positive messages about congressional performance. This was tested with the variable District Partisanship, which gauges the level of demonstrated voting support in a district for the House majority party. It was measured using the two-party vote in the previous two presidential elections.[4] In a district with a majority of Democratic voters the variable would be positive from 1991 through 1994 and negative in 1995 after the Republicans took over the House.

The survey in the previous chapter revealed that a significant number of members believe that constituents' views of the institution do not have an impact on their votes for Congress. These representatives potentially will utilize the "running against Congress" strategy explained by Fenno. In addition, those who do not choose to associate themselves closely with their party but instead run independently are also possible practitioners of this tactic. Among the candidates who see this strategy as an option, the ones most likely to use it are those who are electorally insecure. Secure representatives with little partisan motivation will feel there is no advantage in attacking Congress and may be motivated by a desire to protect the institution's reputation. The desire for institutional maintenance will not be important for vulnerable members because they have a much more compelling goal to pursue. "Running against Congress" may be a practical method of aiding their achievement of this goal.

Gauging a member's sense of security is difficult because this judgment is subjective. Usually, those outside of Congress measure security by looking at the margin by which the representative won in the previous election. But the meaning of this measurement is not unequivocal. A case in point is the debate over whether incumbents became more secure in the 1960s and 1970s as their vote margins increased (Mayhew 1974b). Jacobson (1987) argued that along with the growing vote margins came an increase in the heterogeneity of vote swings, meaning that incumbents had not become more secure.[5] This demonstrates the difficulty of choosing a threshold to distinguish among members who see themselves as secure or vulnerable. Since no indisputable method exists for determining which members consider themselves secure, a common metric often used is the 55 percent threshold. If a representative won with less than this percentage in the previous election (either primary or general) he is considered vulnerable; otherwise he is regarded as being secure. This is the threshold used not only by political scientists, but also by congressional party leaders who pay particular attention to their vulnerable incumbents in order to give them as much help as they need to get reelected. The variable Secure is dichotomous, equal to one for secure members and zero for those who are vulnerable.

There is one other factor that is often regarded as being a significant predictor of members' behavior: seniority. Increasing seniority has been said to decrease a representative's need to pay attention to his constituents, while he also becomes increasingly involved in the institution as a policymaker (Fenno 1978; Cover 1980; Parker 1986). Both decreased obligations to be attentive to constituents and increased involvement in legislating could cause members to become more positive and less negative about Congress. Among those representatives who believe that running against Congress is a good strategy it will be the less senior members, the ones who still need to develop reputations, who will utilize this strategy by sending negative judgments. In addition, those who have served more terms will likely be members who want to maintain a congressional career. If a member wants a long-term career in the House he should have a higher preference for sustaining a good institutional reputation, while "antigovernment" members who are ideologically opposed to many federal programs and are not seeking long careers are more likely to be negative toward Congress. For these reasons the variable Seniority—measured as the number of terms the member has served—should be positively related to members sending positive evaluations of Congress.

It may not be membership in the majority or minority party that is affecting members' messages about Congress, but instead it could be the fact that those in the majority are likely to be winning more legislative battles. The more often a member votes on the winning side of significant legislation, the more opportunities he will have to be positive about congressional activities, especially policy choices. In order to control for this I include a variable called Key Vote Wins that measures the percentage of key votes in a session (as defined by *Congressional Quarterly*) for which the member votes on the winning side. The higher a representative's score on this measure, the greater his probability of sending positive messages. It is possible that this variable could prove to be more significant than partisanship.

All members were placed in one of four categories for each year: negative, positive, mixed, or no messages (as discussed in chap. 3). The dependent variable used to test the model includes three of these categories and ranges from negative, to none, to positive. The small number of members who sent mixed messages were not included in the model estimations.[6] The assumption underlying this ordering is that representatives who are unable to make a strategic choice between being positive or negative will refrain from communicating either message. These are representatives who believe they do not have a clear strategic reason to send one type of message, so they decide it is better not to send any; these members will use other methods of building constituents' trust such as casework or pork-barreling. This is similar to Fenno's claim in *Home Style* that some members choose a style centered around "cultivation of personal relationships," while others choose "a style heavily weighted toward the discussion of policy issues" (1978, 61). Since these representatives choose this strategy because they have some incentives that suggest positive messages and others that recommend negative ones, but neither overwhelms, they are placed in a category in between these two. On account of this natural ordering of categories and because each factor is expected to have an effect across all the levels of the dependent variable, I used ordered probit to estimate the model.[7]

All five variables—Security, Majority Support Score, Seniority, Key Vote Wins, and District Partisanship—are expected to be related positively to the dependent variable, meaning that as its value increases, the likelihood of a member being positive increases, while her probability of being negative decreases. The variable Party was added to the model to test if Democrats and Republicans differed in their judgments after controlling for the other five factors.

RESULTS

All Messages to All Audiences

While the aggregate numbers in chapter 3 suggested that membership in the majority or minority party is very important for predicting whether a member would send positive or negative messages, the model tested here reveals that this factor is highly significant even when considering the impact of several other factors. Table 6 shows the results when including both policy and process messages sent by members in all mail.[8] A representative's Majority Support Score, which measures her partisanship and the strength of her party loyalty, was highly significant in explaining her comments regarding congressional processes.[9] Because of the nonlinear nature of the ordered probit model, first differences are used to demonstrate the degree to which the significant factors had an impact.[10] An average majority party member—one who supported his party 89 percent of the time—was 47.5 percent more likely to send positive messages than a typical minority party member. This indicates a remarkable difference in the behavior of majority and minority party members and strongly supports the claim that "members run with their parties" when communicating with constituents.

Beyond the impact of the Majority Support Score, the partisanship of voters in a district also affects the types of messages that a member sends. The greater the percentage of constituents who support the party

TABLE 6. Factors Affecting the Probability of Sending Negative Messages, No Messages, or Positive Messages in All Mail

	Estimate	Standard Error	Change in Probability of Positive Messages
Cutpoint 1	0.966	0.292	
Cutpoint 2	2.219	0.306	
Majority Support Score	0.0169**	0.0027	47.5%
District Partisanship	0.0020*	0.0015	6.8%
Security	0.372**	0.137	14.6%
Seniority	−0.0006	0.014	—
Key Vote Wins	0.0133**	0.0046	8.7%
Party	0.078	0.157	—

$N = 464$
$*p < 0.10$ $**p < 0.005$

in the majority, the more likely the member is to be positive toward Congress. The average partisanship difference in the congressional districts analyzed was 21 percent, or approximately a 60–40 split between the two major parties. A legislator in a district with 60 percent favoring the congressional majority was about 7 percent more likely to send positive messages than a member in a district with the same percentage supporting the minority. This is not nearly as large an impact as a member's strength of voting support for his party. However, much of the effect of constituents' attitudes, which have their impact through the reelection incentive, is already contained in the Majority Support Score. The significance of District Partisanship shows that the effects of the partisan preferences of district voters go beyond voting behavior on the House floor to the messages representatives send about Congress.

As expected, members who are secure are more likely to be positive than those who are vulnerable. The difference in behavior was very significant, with a secure member found to be 14.6 percent more likely to be positive than a vulnerable one. This suggests that "running against Congress," and not just "running against the majority," is an important strategy that motivates some representatives to send negative messages about the institution. This finding, along with the one concerning District Partisanship, shows that constituents' attitudes have a very significant influence on the messages that members communicate, once again demonstrating the key behavioral impact of the electoral goal. One other variable, Key Vote Wins, was also highly significant; the higher the percentage of key votes for which a member is on the winning side, the more likely he is to be positive. Most important, inclusion of this measure of personal legislative success did not obviate the significance of the other factors and did not overwhelm the substantive impact of partisanship.

The one factor that did not have the impact expected was a member's length of tenure in office. When separate models are run for each party, Seniority is not significant for either one. In addition, when the judgments of members of the majority or minority party were examined separately, neither was affected by the length of tenure (discussed later). Nor is a member's party affiliation a significant factor in predicting judgments after controlling for majority or minority status.

Targeting Audiences

Examining targeted mailings separately from those sent districtwide provides a look at how members may vary their messages when they are addressing a select as opposed to a general audience. Targeted mail serves as a loose approximation of the messages communicated by representatives when they appear in front of particular groups in the district. Analyzing districtwide mail first, we find an almost three-to-one ratio of positive to negative members, with about half of the members not sending any messages about Congress.[11] The results shown in table 7 demonstrate that the same four factors—Majority Support Score, District Partisanship, Security, and Key Vote Wins—were positive and significant for general mail as for all mailings.[12] The Majority Support Score had the largest impact on representatives' messages.[13] An average majority party member was about 26 percent more likely to send positive judgments in districtwide mail than a minority party member who gave average voting support to his party. The measure of District Partisanship shows that a representative of a district with 60 percent favoring the congressional majority was almost 9 percent more likely to send positive messages than someone representing a district with the same percentage supporting the minority. A member who is considered to be electorally secure is 11.5 percent more likely than one who is not secure to send positive messages in districtwide mail. Since comments sent in districtwide mail constitute a large proportion of all messages communicated about Congress, it is not surprising that the results in tables 6 and 7 are so similar.

We can learn more about members' communication strategies for specific audiences by examining targeted mail. The number of members who sent targeted messages about congressional performance is not as large as the number who sent judgments in general mail. The proportion of members who were positive to those who were negative, though, is the same for both types of mail.[14] One important difference to be

TABLE 7. Factors Affecting the Probability of Sending Negative Messages, No Messages, or Positive Messages in Districtwide Mail

	Estimate	Standard Error	Change in Probability of Positive Messages
Cutpoint 1	0.392	0.277	
Cutpoint 2	2.319	0.298	
Majority Support Score	0.010**	0.003	26.2%
District Partisanship	0.0028*	0.002	8.7%
Security	0.326**	0.132	11.5%
Seniority	0.003	0.013	—
Key Vote Wins	0.017**	0.004	10.6%
Party	−0.096	0.148	—

$N = 477$
*$p < 0.025$ **$p < 0.01$

expected involves the District Partisanship variable. Since members are choosing which constituents will receive targeted messages, the aggregate characteristics of voters in a district should not have the impact seen for districtwide mail.

The results in table 8 show that just as when examining messages sent districtwide, the Majority Support Score is the most significant factor in predicting messages sent to targeted audiences.[15] A majority party member who provided average party support is more than 41 percent more likely to send positive judgments than an average minority party member.[16] As expected, unlike with general audience mail, District Partisanship is not positively related to judgments in targeted messages; however, it is a significant negative predictor. A member with an average district partisanship difference favoring the congressional majority was almost 9 percent less likely to send positive messages than a representative of an average district favoring the minority. This indicates important strategic differences in the way that targeted audiences are addressed in regard to messages about congressional performance. The more a constituency opposes the majority, the more likely a representative is to send favorable judgments in targeted mail. This suggests that members will use targeted mail to communicate messages about Congress to constituents in the partisan minority when these comments would be harmful to their reputations if sent to all constituents. It is important to point out that while it is the case that some members will use strategic targeting in this manner, the importance of the Majority Support Score is still extremely high. A good example would be a Republican in 1995 representing a majority Democratic district target-

TABLE 8. Factors Affecting the Probability of Sending Negative Messages, No Messages, or Positive Messages in Targeted Mail

	Estimate	Standard Error	Change in Probability of Positive Messages
Cutpoint 1	0.155	0.272	
Cutpoint 2	2.274	0.293	
Majority Support Score	0.019***	0.0028	41.3%
District Partisanship	−0.003**	0.0013	−8.7%
Security	0.140	0.131	—
Seniority	−0.012	0.013	—
Key Vote Wins	0.006*	0.0045	3.5%
Party	0.261	0.147	—

Note: All tests of statistical significance are one-tailed except for the District Partisanship variable, which is two-tailed because there is no hypothesized relationship with the dependent variable. $N = 482$.

*$p < 0.10$ **$p < 0.05$ ***$p < 0.025$

ing positive messages bolstering his party to those constituents in his district who support the party. Even when it requires careful targeting, members will communicate support for their party.

Key Vote Wins was found to be a significant predictor for targeted messages, but the significance was much lower than for districtwide mail. Consistent with the findings for districtwide mail, Seniority was not a significant predictor of messages sent to targeted audiences. Security was not statistically significant, although the estimate of the effect was positive as expected. Further analysis reveals that electorally secure representatives are less likely than those who are vulnerable to send any judgments of Congress in targeted mail. This lack of variance in security status limits the chances that this factor would be statistically significant.

Policy Messages versus Process Messages

Next, members' messages about congressional policies and processes are examined separately. First I estimate the model for messages about policies. There is a definite skew toward positive judgments, with three times as many members sending favorable messages as negative ones, while almost one-third sent no judgments of policy choices.[17] The results shown in table 9 indicate that the Majority Support Score had the largest impact in predicting the messages members sent about policy.[18] An average majority party member was about 17 percent more likely to send positive judgments about policies than his counterpart in the minority.[19] District Partisanship was positive but narrowly failed a

TABLE 9. Factors Affecting the Probability of Sending Negative Messages, No Messages, or Positive Messages about Policies

	Estimate	Standard Error	Change in Probability of Positive Messages
Cutpoint 1	1.032	0.284	
Cutpoint 2	2.308	0.298	
Majority Support Score	0.016***	0.003	16.7%
District Partisanship	0.0017	0.0014	—
Security	0.305**	0.134	11.9%
Seniority	0.0050	0.014	—
Key Vote Wins	0.015***	0.005	9.5%
Party	0.287*	0.155	11.2%

Note: All tests of statistical significance are one-tailed except for the Party variable, which is two tailed because there is no hypothesized relationship with the dependent variable. $N = 477$.

test of statistical significance. A secure member was about 12 percent more likely to send positive messages than an electorally vulnerable member. Key Vote Wins was once again positive and significant, as would be expected for policy messages, but its impact was only a little more than half that of the Majority Support Score variable. One potentially interesting result is that Republicans were about 11 percent more likely than Democrats to send positive messages about congressional policies. However, this result is driven by the actions of Republicans during one anomalous year. Republicans were much more positive about policies in 1991 than they were in subsequent years during Democratic control (as shown in chap. 3, this vol.). If the messages sent in 1991 are removed from the analysis, there is not a significant difference in behavior between members of the two parties.

In addition to not having as many members making judgments about processes as about policies, there was a noticeable difference in the distribution of members who were positive and negative. Practically an even number of members—about 10.5 percent—are in each category.[20] The very low number of members who sent mixed messages concerning congressional processes is also noteworthy. There is one factor—Key Vote Wins—that was significant for policy judgments but would not be expected to be significant for messages concerning processes. When discussing processes, a member's behavior should not be directly affected by how often he wins or loses on votes.

The results are displayed in table 10, and once again the Majority Support Score is positive and significant.[21] While the level of impact for this factor, as indicated by the first difference, is not as large for process messages as for those about policies, it must be remembered that the

TABLE 10. Factors Affecting the Probability of Sending Negative Messages, No Messages, or Positive Messages about Processes

	Estimate	Standard Error	Change in Probability of Positive Messages
Cutpoint 1	−0.684	0.296	
Cutpoint 2	2.140	0.316	
Majority Support Score	0.0073**	0.0029	5.0%
District Partisanship	0.0029**	0.0015	3.8%
Security	0.231*	0.142	7.6%
Seniority	0.0060	0.014	—
Key Vote Wins	0.0029	0.0049	—
Party	−0.207	0.160	—

$N = 497$
*$p < 0.10$ **$p < 0.025$

percentage of members sending these comments is much smaller.[22] District Partisanship was significant for processes (unlike for policies), indicating another difference between the use of these types of judgments. Comments about processes are affected by the partisanship of constituents to a much higher degree than messages about policies. While support for specific policies can cut across party lines, processes directly reflect upon the party in control of the institution. Thus the partisanship of the people who are receiving the message is of paramount importance when choosing whether to send positive or negative comments regarding processes. As expected, Key Vote Wins was not statistically significant, indicating that the strategies responsible for judgments of processes are distinct from those affecting policies. Consistent with the other models, Seniority was not significant.

Seniority and Cohort Effects

The most surprising finding was that seniority was never a significant predictor of whether members sent positive or negative messages. Contrary to expectations, members do not appear to become more positive about the institution as they spend more time serving in it.[23] There was no difference when looking separately at messages regarding policies and processes; those with higher levels of experience were not more likely to display respect for congressional processes in their messages to constituents. Seniority did not create significant differences for either Democrats or Republicans. All of this indicates that representatives' choices about the messages they send about Congress are not affected by how long they have served in the institution. This suggests that seniority may not have as much of an impact on members' behavior as congressional scholars have thought.

However, because of the prevalence of the belief that more senior members would be more positive about the institution I performed further analyses. Perhaps the apparent differences in behavior between old-timers and newcomers are real, but they are not the result of increasing seniority but instead depend on when a representative entered the institution; that is, representatives' behavior is not impacted by how long they have served in the institution, but instead those who came to Congress in the same time period engage in similar behavior. This would be a cohort effect rather than a seniority effect. The most senior member included in this study was first elected to Congress in 1950. Of course, there are few members from the earlier time periods so it is difficult to get a precise differentiation among members who entered in the 1950s and 1960s.

Clearly the most important demarcation line in at least the past fifty years for American politics and politicians is the 1973 Watergate scandal.[24] The "Watergate babies" of 1974 included a large number of young reformers, mostly Democrats, who were very critical of the government. This class instigated changes in many of the rules regarding the processes used to run the institution; the importance of seniority was decreased, and power was spread more widely among members. This group proved to be not just an anomaly, but the vanguard of a new type of representative who was much more likely to be an individualistic policy entrepreneur. As Loomis explains in *The New American Politician*:

> Beginning with the class of '74, a new generation of leaders rushed to the fore of American politics and brought with them a new way of doing business. The central elements of this new style include expertise and the willingness to work hard, often at the expense of comity, collegiality, and compromise. (1988, 28)

It may be that the anecdotes about young Turks who do not respect the institution are not referring to a generalized seniority effect, but to this new cohort. If this is the case, members elected in the post-Watergate era would demonstrate a greater likelihood of being negative than those who entered office prior to this event.[25]

There is one other year that stands out when analyzing recent changes in Congress: 1994. After forty years in the minority the Republican party gained 52 seats and captured control of the House. This surprising outcome was widely viewed as a strong declaration of public dissatisfaction with the way the institution was being operated. The new members who entered after the 1994 election, particularly Republicans, likely found it in their interest to show that they were succeeding in changing the way the institution operated. Therefore, representatives elected in this year—especially but not only Republicans—should be more positive about Congress in 1995. This is exactly what was found when analyzing this group of members. However, it is not clear whether this will continue to be a trait of this cohort or whether the positive messages were simply the immediate impact of being elected in a revolution. Because of the uniqueness of the 1994 class it was not included in the analysis of the pre- and post-Watergate cohorts.

To test whether there is a significant difference in the messages sent by members who entered the institution before and after 1974, the model was estimated with the Seniority variable replaced by a dichotomous variable indicating whether the member is part of the post-Watergate cohort. Estimating the model for all evaluation messages indicates that the post-Watergate cohort was not more likely to communicate negative messages about the institution. However, this is a situation in which it is especially helpful to consider representatives' comments about processes separate from those about policies. Some of the major complaints from members both during and after Watergate have been about congressional processes. I have already shown that when we examine process and policy messages independently there are different factors that predict who will be positive and who will be negative. Therefore, the model with the cohort variable was run again looking at each of these types of messages separately.

Not surprisingly, the results when looking only at policy messages were the same as when considering all communication (since comments about policy make up a large percentage of all messages); there was no difference in behavior between the pre- and post-Watergate cohorts. However, examining only process statements reveals that post-Watergate entrants into Congress were significantly more likely to be negative (see table 11). The first difference indicates that members of the new guard were more than 15 percent more likely to be negative in messages about processes. This is a very large impact when considering how few members send process judgments to their constituents. Less senior members do behave very differently from more senior members in this one aspect of communication. It is not a result of members changing their messages as they spend more time in Congress, rather the representatives who have entered post-Watergate are more likely to bash institutional processes.

TABLE 11. Factors Affecting the Probability of Sending Negative Messages, No Messages, or Positive Messages about Processes, with Cohort Variable

	Estimate	Standard Error
Cutpoint 1	−1.076	0.327
Cutpoint 2	1.792	0.338
Majority Support Score	0.00663*	0.00298
District Partisanship	0.0029*	0.0015
Security	0.300	0.133
Post-Watergate Cohort	−0.419**	0.162
Key Vote Wins	0.0033	0.00496
Party	−0.233	0.157

$N = 497$
$*p < 0.025$ $**p < 0.005$

While 1974 is usually focused upon as the pivotal year, the "Watergate babies" were mostly Democrats. It would be instructive to examine the two parties separately and see if a similar cohort effect occurred for Republicans and whether it was during the same time period. Examining the internal history of the congressional Republican party indicates that the year that marked a dividing line between the old and new guard occurred later than 1974. It was the Republican class of 1980 (along with the smaller class of 1978) that "formed the GOP equivalent of the Democrats' 75 'Watergate Babies'" (Hook 1988, 2263). The 52 Republicans elected during the Reagan Revolution "thrust House Republicans into a newly aggressive role" (2262). The attitude of many of these representatives was reflected in their class president Hank Brown (CO) who said, "My goal was to change the institution" (2263). This was a new guard of confrontationalists who had an attitude different from the old guard of compromisers. Soon thereafter, in 1983, Newt Gingrich formed the Conservative Opportunity Society (COS), which touted the Republican confrontational strategy. While for Democrats 1974 may have been the turning point, for Republicans it was likely that 1980 marked the time when members became more negative about the institution, particularly the way in which the institution operated. Therefore when the parties are analyzed separately this is the year that is used as the dividing line between old and new Republicans.

When the model was run separately for each party, the cohort variable was not found to be significant when looking at policy messages, but the results were different for process statements. Both the post-Watergate Democrats and post–Reagan Revolution Republicans were significantly more likely to be negative than their more senior counterparts in their parties. The "new guard" of the Republican party was 13.4 percent more likely to be negative than those members elected before 1980.[26] The confrontationalist post-1980 Republicans believed in attacking the institutional processes much more than their compromising seniors. The post-Watergate Democrats were found to be 10.1 percent more likely to communicate negative messages about congressional processes than members elected before that pivotal event.[27] Further analysis reveals that these were indeed the critical turning-point years for the two parties.

MEMBERS' VIEWS OF THE FINDINGS

These findings were presented to members of Congress and congressional staff to get their reactions and to seek the explanations they had to offer for some of the results (more details about these interviews are contained in chap. 2). None of the twenty-two members interviewed was surprised that membership in the majority or minority party was the most significant factor in predicting positive and negative judgments. What was most interesting were the reactions to a critical question that arose out of this finding—to what extent do parties, specifically party leaders, have an impact on the content of messages communicated to constituents?

Impact of Party Leaders on Members' Messages

Both parties provide a variety of resources that may influence the content of their members' communication. Leaders spend a significant amount of time and energy encouraging and facilitating the use of party rhetoric (see Lipinski 2001b). The parties hold weekly meetings for press secretaries to apprise them of current party messages and the events being held to promote these, along with providing suggestions on how to garner local press coverage. Staff briefings are held to keep party members on the same page when taking positions and explaining them to the public. Weekly Democratic Caucus and Republican Conference meetings focus members on current issues and discuss communication strategies. In addition to these meetings, the leadership message operations disseminate a number of different publications that highlight issues, actions, or events that the party wants to promote. Both parties have leadership groups that encourage and coordinate the communication of partisan messages on the House floor.

In order to help their members communicate party rhetoric to their constituents, the Democratic Policy Committee provides a packet of information to take home every weekend. This publication called the *Weekender* contains materials explaining party rhetoric on various current issues, gives useful statistics to communicate to constituents, and even includes examples of articles that can be put into mailings. All of these are ways for the leadership to make it as easy as possible for their members to send the messages the party leaders prefer. The Republican Conference publishes a similar but much less extensive packet for their members to take home each weekend called the *Boarding Pass*. The Republicans generally put more emphasis on communication in the districts during extended recesses.

While party leaders expend this high level of effort, it is not clear how much direct impact it has on the messages that their members send. To the survey question "How often, if ever, do you follow suggestions [from your party on communicating with constituents]?" 6 percent of the members responded "very often," and 42 percent said "once in a while." These responses suggest that leadership efforts have an impact on the communication activities of about half of their members. Representatives like to maintain their autonomy, so this can make it difficult at times for party leaders to receive cooperation. All incumbent representatives have been elected at least once—usually many times—so they believe that they know their constituents and how to appeal to them. The sentiments of many I interviewed was summed up by a fifth-term Democrat who said, "I know my constituents better than the leadership or the DNC [Democratic National Committee]!" This feeling was echoed more forcefully (and less diplomatically) by the Chief of Staff for another Democrat who said, "Members know what has appeal in their districts better than any yahoo around [Capitol Hill]." This independence may be overemphasized to some degree, however, since few members want to be viewed as mouthpieces for the party and unsympathetic to constituents.

In the interviews, members emphasized that the most important consequence of leadership efforts is to provide useful information that otherwise would not have been available. Even if a member does not include a party-produced article or directly quote the party line, the content of her messages may still be influenced by leaders. The effect can be as simple as convincing a member to choose to talk about an issue of interest to her constituents that allows her to be positive about what the party has done (or negative about the opposition). One Democratic member said that the "party is helpful because they have the staff to keep track of ideas" and "[I] sometimes pick up on these ideas." Another Democratic representative said that "the party gives raw information," but the member has to decide on specific messages to send to constituents. Polling data was cited as helpful information that would not be available to members were it not for the party.

While the parties may provide useful information that can help shape members' messages, there is definitely a limit to the influence that party leaders can have over the content of what their members will send. It is highly unlikely that party leaders could overcome the influence of the electoral goal if constituents' attitudes provide a member with the incentive not to send messages supporting the party. As a Democrat explained:

> The party does give out some direction, some information, suggestions on what to talk about in your newsletters; I suppose if you come from a traditional historic Democratic district they would be advantageous to use but coming from a district that is probably more Republican than Democrat I would not think of using any of the issues.

This shows that concerns about constituents will most often trump leadership efforts when it comes to using the various resources that the party offers for constructing messages.

There were a few members I spoke with from both parties that lamented the fact that many of their colleagues do not echo the party line. They complained about the lack of cohesiveness among their members. An eight-term Democrat paraphrased Will Rogers when he stated, "We're Democrats, we don't belong to an organized party." A Republican claimed that trying to lead his membership is "like herding cats."[28] These were members who had strong ideological or leadership interests in their party and thus an extraordinary desire to have the party message repeated. It is difficult to say if these representatives would ever be satisfied with the level of party cooperation in the American system.

Party Leadership and Messages Judging Congress

The messages that leaders give to their members are undoubtedly chosen to aid the party. But do these party strategies include encouraging members to send comments judging congressional performance? I asked Democrats whether they were encouraged by their leaders or their colleagues to be supportive of Congress prior to 1995 when they were in the majority. Although the Democrats had remained in power for many years while public approval of Congress was low, I reasoned that there may have been some fear that this situation could eventually hurt the party. The Democrats I spoke with offered differing opinions as to whether or not this was the case, but most agreed that they remembered the leadership urging members to be positive about Congress. One Democrat, who has been in Congress since 1986, said that "the leadership was always trying to sell [being positive]." He emphasized that "[Speaker] Foley was always telling Democrats to be positive." A staff member very familiar with Foley's reign as Speaker echoed this member's statement. He said that he remembers Foley and other representatives encouraging their colleagues in the Democratic Caucus to be positive about the accomplishments of Congress.

After Bill Clinton was elected president in 1992 the Democratic Party faced the opportunities and responsibilities that arise under unified government. While congressional Democrats no longer had a Republican president who would obstruct their preferred policies, this also meant that they did not have someone to shift blame to for any apparent shortcomings of government. This gave Democrats in Congress another reason to try to build their reputation of running the institution well. A

Democratic member elected in 1992 said that when he arrived in Washington he was encouraged by the leadership to be positive because "we were in charge." This representative understood this behavior as simply "the way leadership works." Another representative who came into Congress as Clinton was elected noted a "leadership effort to suggest ... success or failure would be attributed to us." This demonstrates that the party leaders placed an even greater emphasis on getting their members to send messages supporting Congress and Democrats' success in 1993 and 1994. But some Democrats noted a change in their leadership's behavior even earlier than this. A long-serving Democrat said that party leaders began in the mid-1980s to emphasize the need for members to be loyal to the party in the messages that they communicated to the public. This representative said:

> They [the leadership] were trying to get the membership to sing from one hymn book, that the Democratic Congress and the Democratic leadership were doing all the right things, all the things that the American people wanted. They [the leadership] didn't want to have any discouraging words in their members' newsletters about the Democratic Congress or some of the Democratic legislation because they felt it would be hurting their leadership positions.

All of these Democrats admitted that they felt the pressure to be positive, or at least not be negative, about Congress when their party was in charge. This demonstrates a concerted effort among party leaders in the majority to encourage their members to run with Congress.

Between the 102d and 103d Congresses there was a significant drop in the number of Republicans sending positive messages. The two factors most likely responsible for this were the Democrats' capture of the White House and changes in strategy among congressional Republicans (see chap. 3, this vol.). Many Republican members, asked how they would explain this shift in messages, cited the change in control of the White House. As one Republican said, "We lost the bully pulpit." Another explained, "When you control the White House you feel you can do more." Even though they were in the minority in both houses of Congress Republicans felt they still possessed some power through their party's control of the presidency. When this was lost after twelve years, congressional Republicans felt that they had little to be positive about in government.

The 1992–93 time period was also pivotal in regard to changes occurring inside the congressional Republican Party. As discussed earlier, rising Republican star Newt Gingrich had been urging the party to engage in a strategy of attacking Congress in an effort to end Democratic control. By the time Congress convened in 1993 the party was largely under the control of members who ascribed to the confrontationalist strategy. A number of changes occurred during the party's organizational meeting in December 1992.

> Aided by a freshman class bent on change, the activists dethroned the incumbent Republican Conference chairman, retained control over every other top post below Minority Leader Robert H. Michel . . . and curbed the power of members to free-lance with the Democratic majority. (Kuntz 1992, 3781)

The message sent to all ranking members was that "they need to be more aggressive in confronting Democrats and more willing to heed the conference's conservative proclivities" (Kuntz 1992, 3781).

In my interviews I asked members if they saw a shift in attitudes among Republicans around this time. One Republican said that in 1993 "the feeling started to grow that Gingrich was on the way up" and because his "whole movement and tone was negative, the troops followed." By the fall of 1993 it was clear that Gingrich would be the new leader of the Republicans in the 104th Congress when Robert H. Michel retired. At that time it was said that "Michel's retirement . . . will clear the way for the party hierarchy to be dominated by the confrontational brand of Republicanism that is in ascendance and makes Michel's consensus-oriented style seem like an anachronism" (Hook 1993, 2714). Gingrich's strategy had certainly been noted on the other side of the aisle also. A Democrat I interviewed noted that "Newt Gingrich's policy was to oppose." The very negative, anti-Congress message propounded by Gingrich since the late 1980s had been gaining more and more adherents among Republicans, picked up speed in 1992, and had largely taken hold of the party by 1993.

By the time of the 1994 election, "running against Congress" became one of the favored themes promoted internally by Republican strategists to party members. According to one Republican I interviewed, the National Republican Congressional Committee—the party's congressional campaign organization—advised members in their meetings that it might be useful to run against Congress. While the leadership was promoting this electoral strategy, the rank and file began to believe that after forty years in the minority the goal of taking over the House was possible. This led more Republicans to take up this strategy. A Republican I interviewed noted that in 1993 his party was "driving the issue to take over because we were starting to smell that we could win if we drove it."

There is one more factor that should not be overlooked when looking at the shift by Republicans away from positive messages in 1992 and 1993. I have demonstrated the significant impact that public attitudes have on the messages members send. Representatives will cater what they say about the institution to what their constituents already think. A Democrat I interviewed suggested that the presidential candidacy of Ross Perot not only fed on but also increased the level of antigovernment sentiment in the public. Faced with this attitude among constituents, it made sense for many Republicans to shift their messages about Congress. The strategy that Newt Gingrich and other Republicans had been urging for a number of years found a more receptive audience because public attitudes encouraged these types of messages.

Effect of Electoral Security on Members' Messages about Congress

Another question I explored in my interviews with members was their understanding of the effect of security on members' messages about Congress. Most members clearly expected that electorally vulnerable members were more likely to be negative. Their reasons often were based on the presumption that sending negative messages is an especially good method for building trust with constituents. An eighth-term Democrat commenting on the actions of insecure members said:

> They are trying to build upon a positive image that they have in their own district; they don't want to have to try to make excuses for why people may not view the institution that favorably. By attacking the institution of Congress members are saying "it's not my fault, it's the institution's fault, don't take it out on me; I agree with you that Congress did a terrible thing here and a terrible thing there—I voted against it but unfortunately that terrible majority prevailed."

This is very similar to the way Fenno described members' thoughts about "running against Congress" in *Home Style*. But this representative said that he expected vulnerable members to be more likely to communicate this type of message. Other members said that in most districts there is a group of voters to whom the legislator can appeal by attacking the institution. If a member is vulnerable he will want to make sure he appeals to this anti-Congress group. The comments made by these representatives are summed up well by a third-term Democrat who stated:

> If [a member] has trouble holding a district he is more likely to criticize because it plays to the crowd; some significant number [of constituents] is usually upset with Congress and by criticizing Congress [the member] is playing up to this anger.

Other representatives talked about how negative messages are much better at gaining the attention of constituents. A seventh-term Republican explained that because negative messages are "more volatile and attention-getting . . . they [produce the] smell of blood and shake things up." A second-term Democrat said that because it is "part of human nature to respond to negative messages" it makes sense for members—especially insecure ones—to send these types of messages. Vulnerable members need to be more prepared for the attacks of their opponents and have to do whatever they can to immunize themselves from expected charges. A staff member explained a communication strategy utilized by some vulnerable incumbents: "You don't want to give an opponent an opening; [you can] preempt an opponent's attack [on the member] for being part of the institution since outsiders will usually try to attack in this way."

One other reason for vulnerable members to be negative about Congress did not involve the strategic value of the messages. Instead, it focuses on the psychological impact of representing a marginal district. A four-term Republican said that a member who "has had to fight and scrape to get here usually has had to take a more aggressive position; these members have more anger and aggressiveness."[29] It is not that these members have had to be strategically negative about Congress to get elected, but as they constantly battle to keep their seats they become very negative about everything including Congress. This psychological rather than strategic explanation for vulnerable members being negative is difficult to prove or disprove.

The Nonfinding Regarding Seniority

The most surprising nonfinding in my analysis was that seniority was not a significant predictor of members' messages. As I have shown, however, there is a cohort effect with the "new guard" in both parties being more likely to be negative about congressional processes. Most representatives I interviewed expected that greater seniority would mean a higher likelihood of sending positive evaluations of the institution. Members' expectations, though, were not based on their own strategic considerations but rather beliefs about personal choices they see arising out of the circumstances accompanying different levels of seniority.

One senior (seventh-term) Republican said, "Usually young Turks come in to kick ass," and a junior (second-term) Republican stated that members with little seniority are usually "griping because they don't have power." These representatives believed that these attitudes would be translated into the communication of negative messages about Congress. A senior Democrat (eighth-term) said, "I would have expected more senior members to be more positive because they have more respect for the institution and they can get more done because they have been there longer." A couple of members stated that they would expect seniority to lead to more positive messages because seniority produces a greater "stake in the institution." Again, these members did not cite strategy but instead spoke about attitudes causing more senior members to be more positive about Congress in their messages. The evidence presented in this book suggests that the strategic expectations suggested by congressional scholars and the attitudinal expectations offered by representatives are not fulfilled in members' behavior.

A few members did offer possible explanations for this nonfinding in regard to seniority. A fifth-term Republican suggested that one reason members may get more negative as time goes on is because they get "burned out" and they see "friends leave Congress." These factors causing negativity counteract the others cited earlier that would make members more positive about the institution. Another representative contended that the "older guys are frustrated because the rules have changed dramatically and they are not the exalted rulers." That is, seniority no longer grants the power and respect that it once did, and this change gives more senior members fewer reasons to be positive. Other members explained that being positive or negative is often a reflection of individuals' personalities and "personal attitudes" rather than a function of seniority. One member gave the example that "[Rep. John] Dingell [in his twenty-first term] is 'still excited' while others quickly become unhappy." All of these may explain to some degree seniority's lack of impact on members' communication about Congress.

DISCUSSION

This chapter showed the significant impact that partisanship has on the messages that members send evaluating congressional performance. A member's strength of support for his party is clearly the most important predictor of whether he will send positive or negative messages about Congress, and the level of this impact was shown to be very high. The effect of parties was also demonstrated by the impact that voter partisanship has in shaping the messages that members send to their constituents. Even when controlling for a representative's electoral security and the level of success he has in voting on the floor—both of which are also important predictors—partisanship still stands out. Whether it is communicating with all members in the district or with specific audiences, members will "run with their parties" by sending the appropriate message about congressional performance. These results fulfill the predictions of congressional party government theories that focus on leadership attempts to succeed in the legislative arena in order to build the party record. When observing the permanent campaign we see members behaving just as expected in sending messages promoting their party and tying themselves to it.

Now that I have shown and explained the content of the messages regarding Congress that members are communicating to their constituents, I turn to the question of whether messages have consequences. In order to have any effect communication first has to be received and remembered by the intended recipient. But little is known about the extent to which members can communicate strategic messages to their constituents. In the next chapter I test whether members can successfully send a particular piece of information crucial to the representative-constituent connection—the position they have taken on specific votes.

PART II CONSEQUENCES

5 MEMBERS' SUCCESS IN COMMUNICATING INFORMATION TO CONSTITUENTS

> *I wanted my constituents to know how I voted.*
> —Senior Democrat explaining why he advertised his vote on the Persian Gulf War Use of Force Resolution

We have examined the content of and motivations for the messages members send to their constituents regarding the performance of Congress. Most studies of congressional communication stop at this point and either implicitly or explicitly presume that this behavior has the intended impact. However, there is little empirical evidence regarding the success representatives have communicating with constituents. In this chapter I take the next step and begin testing the effects of members' communication.

HOW AND WHY TO TEST THE COMMUNICATION OF VOTES

In order to have any consequences, messages first have to be received and retained. Ideally we could directly test this in regard to members' messages about congressional performance. Unfortunately this is extremely difficult with the available data and methods. Opinions regarding Congress are shaped by countless sources over an indeterminable time period. It would be hard to measure the impact of members' communication separate from other influences. In addition, it would be tricky to delineate cause and effect. Instead, I test whether a member can successfully communicate to constituents the position she has taken on specific votes. In democratic theory it is often considered essential for citizens to know the votes their representatives have cast in order to make informed choices in elections.[1] But democratic theory is not what members of Congress consider when they decide whether or not to publicize how they have voted. The member quoted in the epigraph believed that it was very important for his constituents to know how he voted on the Persian Gulf War Use of Force Resolution. He thought that this information would build his reputation and help him get reelected. The member made the strategic decision to put forth the effort to publicize his position to help achieve this goal.

Studying members' messages and constituents' knowledge regarding votes is one of the best techniques for testing whether communication can be successful. Because votes are discrete pieces of information it is easier to measure members' impact on what their constituents know. On the transmission side, it is possible to study representatives' communication and gauge whether they made the effort to inform constituents about their position on a particular vote. On the reception side, constituents' knowledge can be measured using available individual-level survey data. Other factors affecting the likelihood of a respondent knowing a representative's vote can be controlled for by utilizing a previously constructed model. All of this facilitates a good measure of the degree to which members can successfully communicate chosen information to their constituents.

I test the ability of members to influence constituents' knowledge of their positions on two high-salience votes—the 1991 Persian Gulf War Use of Force Resolution and the 1993 Budget-Reconciliation Conference Report. The American National Election Study's (ANES) 1990–1991 Panel Study of the Political Consequences of War and the 1993 Pilot Study include questions that tap into constituents' knowledge of their representative's vote on these two major issues. Since these surveys were conducted in an off year they are free from the context of congressional campaigns; therefore, constituents' knowledge is not unevenly affected by the presence, quality, or tactics of challengers.

In this chapter I once again use the content of mass mailings to measure whether or not members attempted to communicate how they voted on these issues. The analysis in this chapter serves not only as a method of examining whether members can successfully transmit their chosen messages to constituents, but it is also a good test of whether mass mailings are legitimate proxies for the messages members send through all their communication. If the evidence shows that legislators can successfully communicate messages regarding votes, it will suggest that the content of mail is a good proxy for all of a member's communication.

Members' Strategies in Publicizing or Not Publicizing Votes

Before analyzing the impact of these messages it is essential to examine why members choose to publicize or not publicize votes on major issues. The reasons vary, as the contexts differ depending on the member and the vote. But it is the reelection goal that motivates all members' choices as they make strategic decisions that are intended to build or maintain support among constituents. Because of the equity of available resources for sending mass mailings, the main determinant of whether or not a vote is publicized is strategic calculation; that is, members ask themselves, "Would it help me build trust with my constituents to communicate how I voted on this issue?" If the member believes that discussing his position on a vote will aid him in achieving his electoral goal, he will endeavor to communicate this information in every manner possible including use of mass mailings across his entire district.

Reasons for Publicizing

There are two main reasons members publicize their votes: credit-taking and explanation. First, a member may want her constituents to know how she voted so that she will be given credit for a stance that she believes will be looked upon favorably. In this case no explanation of the issue is necessary. Second, the member may feel that she needs to explain to her constituents why she voted the way she did (for an examination of members' explanations see Bianco 1994). A member will feel the need to expend the effort to take credit for a vote when she believes that her constituents may not know her position, but explanations are sometimes more necessary when the representative believes that her constituents do know her vote. This is one of the key differences in the decision making behind these two reasons for publicizing votes.

In my survey of members I explored their rationales for publicizing or not publicizing votes on the 1991 Persian Gulf War Use of Force Resolution and the 1993 Budget-Reconciliation Conference Report.[2] Members' reasons for publicizing fell into both the credit-taking and explanation categories. An important difference between these two votes was the level of ambiguity about the consequences of passing the legislation. Prior to the vote on the Use of Force Resolution it was clear that approval would open the door to military confrontation. Soon after the vote was taken, the war began and was quickly brought to a widely agreed upon successful conclusion. On the other hand, the projected impact of the budget package was much more contentious, and the arguments over the results continued long after the vote was taken. While the Republicans disparaged the budget as a tax increase, the Democrats lauded it as deficit reduction. This meant that there was more latitude and need for explanation of the budget vote. Members' responses to the survey question "Why did/didn't you advertise your position in your newsletters?" indicate that explanations were more prevalent on the budget vote than on the war vote.

Most of the members who said that they publicized their position on the Gulf War resolution did not say that they needed to explain their vote, but that they mentioned it because it was a "big issue." One Democrat said that he publicized his vote because "questions of war are the most serious issues upon which Congress can vote." Others stressed—in the words of one member—that constituents "deserved to know." The reasoning behind these justifications is probably not only that the vote was important or that constituents had a right to know, but that the member thought that sending this message helped build constituents' trust. Some members were more straightforward about their strategic reasons for proclaiming their vote. The senior Democrat quoted in the epigraph of this chapter is one example.

The 1993 Budget-Reconciliation vote had a higher incidence of members who claimed in the survey that they explained their vote rather than simply taking credit for it, though some did claim that they were only credit-taking. One Democrat who voted against his party's president declared that he advertised his position "to help with the voters." Another Democrat who voted in favor explained that he publicized his vote because "I was proud of my vote." More prevalent, however, were members who said that they publicized the vote to explain their position and/or the legislation. One senior Democrat said directly, "I wanted to explain my position to my constituents," while another stated, "[I wanted to] inform constituents of my position and why I voted the way I voted." Other representatives decided that they needed to explain the content and consequences of the budget. A Democrat who voted for passage said, "This was an extremely controversial vote and I needed to clear up many of the misleading statements that had been made about so-called tax increases." These members assumed that the messages they sent could improve constituents' opinions regarding the budget and thus aid their own reputations.

Members' Position Statements

When examining a member's statement publicizing a vote it is not always possible to distinguish whether her purpose was to take credit or to explain. It is clear that a member is simply taking credit for a popular position when she provides no explanation. However, a member who strategically does not feel a need to explain why her vote was correct may still place her statement in an article that can be construed as an explanation. This means that although a content analysis can reveal who did and did not give an explanation of a vote, it cannot be used to discern whether a member's purpose is to increase the number of constituents who know how she voted or to convince them that her position was the correct one. Thus it would not be legitimate to analyze members in separate credit-taking and explaining categories based on the public statements they made.

My analysis of position statements on the Gulf War resolution revealed that about one-quarter of the representatives did not provide any explanation for their vote. This was especially true for members who supported the resolution. On page 1 of a newsletter Jack Fields (R-TX) stated, "I supported legislation giving the president the authority to use force to implement those United Nations resolutions." Similarly, on the front page of a newsletter sent in May 1991 Bill Paxon (R-NY) said, "I was the only WNY'er [western New Yorker] who voted to authorize President Bush to use force if Iraq refused to withdraw from Kuwait." Paxon did not feel the need to explain the reasoning behind his position, but he wanted to make sure that his constituents gave him the credit he deserved for being the only representative in his area to cast this vote.

Many supporters of the resolution did offer an explanation for their position. In August 1991, Dana Rohrabacher (R-CA) stated,

> I strongly supported President Bush's request for Congressional authorization to use force to kick Saddam Hussein out of Kuwait. Our troops were in the desert and deserved nothing less than our unqualified backing.

Even statements such as this one that included a brief explanation did not give an elaborate assertion of the value of the position. It was presumed that constituents knew about the war and were happy with its conclusion.

Providing an explanation for the Persian Gulf War vote was certainly more important for those who opposed the resolution. Floyd Flake (D-NY), on the front page of his spring 1991 newsletter, accounted for his vote with this statement:

> I opposed the resolution to go to war because war did not seem to be the appropriate solution for the Persian Gulf at that time. I preferred giving sanctions an opportunity to work. I did not want to send our young American troops into battle and ask them to make the ultimate sacrifice for their country if other options were available.

Explaining her position in a newsletter Cardiss Collins (D-IL) said, "I remain concerned that the peaceful alternatives to war were not sufficiently explored by the President prior to launching Desert Storm."

Members' position statements regarding the Budget-Reconciliation vote were noticeably different from those concerning the war vote. There were a few members who simply stated their position on this legislation with little explanation. One such member was Robert Torricelli (D-NJ) who listed the budget along with other key issues voted on during the session on page 2 of his December 1993 newsletter.

> Vote: Yes Budget Reconciliation—President Clinton's economic plan calling for $496 billion in deficit reduction over five years and a freeze in discretionary spending at 1993 levels through fiscal year 1998. Passed 218–216

It should be noted that even this position statement made sure that this legislation was described as a deficit reduction plan.

Typical among Republicans, all of whom voted in opposition, was a sharp attack leveled against the alleged effects of the budget plan. On page 1 of an October 1993 newsletter, Doug Bereuter (R-NE) declared:

> I opposed the Clinton economic plan and voted against . . . the modified conference report version which passed the House on August 5, 1993. The imbalanced reliance on additional new taxes, especially those on small business, in combination with the anticipated huge new costs of health care reform, will probably abort or hurt economic recovery, kill more jobs than it creates, and give us a higher deficit at the end of the five year period than we have today.

Similarly, Steve Horn (R-CA) in his 1993 year-end newsletter stated:

> I opposed the Clinton tax increase plan because the tax increase will hurt economic growth and most of the promised spending cuts will never materialize. By the President's own admission, his plan will never balance the budget.

Both of these statements not only gave the member's position, but also asserted reasons for why this was such a bad proposal.

Just as strongly as many Republicans attacked the budget, some Democrats who voted in favor explained its virtues. On the front page of his fall 1993 newsletter, Bruce Vento (D-MN) asserted:

$500 billion in deficit reduction will be achieved over five years by *changing our national priorities—investing in our future, investing in our families, attaining improved tax fairness, and cutting national spending*. I supported this new policy path which calls for **$255 billion in spending reductions and $241 billion in revenue increases**— 90% of which would be paid by those individuals making more than $100,000 per year. (Emphasis in original)

There were other members who did not claim that the budget was either unconditionally good or bad. Instead they explained their decision making. For example, Pete Stark (D-CA) in a September 1993 newsletter discussed his vote as a tough decision.

Some claim it is the key to the future, some say it is a disaster. In truth it was the best plan available to reduce the deficit—and I voted for it. It reduced the deficit and did it more equitably than any other plan on the table.

The choice to explain support by strongly defending the plan or by discussing it as a difficult decision likely depended on the member's perception of constituents' attitudes and the level of trust she had established in her district.

Reasons for Not Publicizing

The main reason for members *not* publicizing their positions is that they believe they will not help or may hurt their electoral chances if they communicate with constituents regarding their vote. Since it is often assumed that members have a duty to inform constituents about their votes, they understandably would be reluctant to admit that they refrained from discussing a vote in order to avoid a potential backlash. But some members who responded to the survey acknowledged that they strategically chose not to publicize their position. A Democrat from a relatively conservative district who voted in favor of the 1993 Budget-Reconciliation Conference Report said that he did not talk about his position because "it was not a popular position!" (exclamation point included by member). Another Democrat who voted in favor of the budget offered this explanation for why he didn't publicize his vote: "because of the purely partisan nature of the vote—i.e., all GOP [representatives] voted against, all Democrats for—I felt all [my constituents] knew and publicizing my position might anger my GOP [constituents] who vote for me." These are two excellent examples of how electoral considerations cause members to prefer that their constituents do not know how they voted on an issue.

Another reason that some members do not publicize how they vote is that they believe their position has already been communicated to their constituents by the news media. All else equal, members do not want to expend the resources needed to communicate a message if they do not feel that the effort is necessary. A few members who responded to my survey acknowledged that they did not have to publicize their vote because their position was already well known, particularly on account of media coverage. In regard to the 1991 Persian Gulf War Use of Force Resolution, one Democrat stated, "I didn't have to [advertise my position], I talked about it on TV." Another said the "local press covered it well enough!" (exclamation point included by member). There were also members who said that their position on the 1993 Budget-Reconciliation vote was known by constituents, and therefore they didn't have to publicize it. A junior Democrat said she didn't have to put forth the effort because "my vote was advertised by the daily newspapers that serve my district," while another said, "My position was widely reported in the news media."

THE MODEL

Variables from the Existing Model of Perceptual Accuracy of Votes

In order to test whether members' communication efforts have an effect on what their constituents know, it is important to consider other factors that influence such knowledge. Alvarez and Gronke (1996) constructed a model of factors likely to explain the situations in which a survey respondent is able to correctly identify his representative's stance on a major issue. One set of variables measures characteristics of the respondent: media attentiveness, level of political information, political efficacy, education, and salience of the war. Other variables measure member characteristics: ideological extremity and tenure. The final set measures interactions between a respondent and his representative: the respondent's evaluation of his representative, partisan agreement/disagreement, and the respondent's perceived agreement/disagreement with his representative on the vote (see appendix E for explanation of variables). Alvarez and Gronke tested this model using ANES survey data on public perceptions of their representative's position on the Persian Gulf War Use of Force Resolution.

Variables Created for This Test

The model I test incorporates the Alvarez and Gronke model plus two new factors—the variable of primary interest measuring whether or not a respondent's representative publicized her vote and another gauging the level of geographic congruence between the respondent's congressional district and media markets. In order to determine whether a respondent's representative publicized her position on a piece of legislation, a content analysis was conducted on all the districtwide mailings sent by that member during the year in which the vote took place.[3] This was done for every member of Congress whose district included at least one respondent in the relevant ANES sample.

A survey respondent whose representative publicized her position on the pertinent legislation in any districtwide mailing during the year in which the vote took place was categorized as having been the target of a member's publicity effort (coded 1). Otherwise the respondent was considered to have not been sent such a message by his representative, and the publicity effort variable was coded 0.[4] The publicity effort is coded as a dichotomous variable because it measures whether or not the member attempted to inform her constituents about her position through various media. More precise measures of the intensity of publicity efforts are not possible.[5]

As explained earlier, it is not possible to discern from a content analysis whether a member's purpose was credit-taking or explaining, so messages cannot be coded along this dimension. It is important to note that when the circumstances around a vote elicit an exceptional number of explanations, problems occur in the measurement of members' publicity efforts. The purpose of a credit-taking message is to inform those who might not know the member's stance, while explanations are often given when constituents are already assumed to know the representative's position. When these two different efforts cannot be delineated, there is a bias against finding that members have the ability to effectively communicate their position.

An important factor not included in the Alvarez and Gronke model is the level of geographic congruence between congressional districts and media markets. Using the 1980 American National Election Study (ANES) survey, Campbell, Alford, and Henry (1984) demonstrate that higher congruence results in greater media exposure and name recognition for representatives in their districts. Niemi, Powell, and Bicknell (1986) also find in the 1978 ANES data that higher levels of congruence result in greater recall and recognition of the representative's name.[6] This occurs because the fewer media markets which cover a district, and the fewer districts in those media markets, the more likely a district's representative is to receive coverage from the local news media. Greater amounts of coverage translate into constituents having more knowledge about their member. All of this evidence suggests that it is important to control for the level of congruence of congressional districts and media markets when predicting constituents' knowledge about their representative's vote.

Dependent Variables

The American National Election Study's 1990–1991 Panel Study of the Political Consequences of War and 1993 Pilot Study included questions that measured constituents' knowledge of their representative's vote on the two issues I examine. The 1991 survey included respondents residing in 122 congressional districts, while in 1993 there were 120 districts with at least one respondent. In both of the surveys respondents were asked to recall or guess how their representative voted on a particular piece of legislation (in 1991 the Persian Gulf War Use of Force Resolution and in 1993 the Budget-Reconciliation Conference Report). From each survey I developed a dependent variable that measures a respondent's accuracy when stating the vote. This variable is dichotomous since the respondent was either incorrect (coded 0) or correct (coded 1) about his representative's position. Therefore I use probit to estimate the models.

RESULTS

Effect of Media Market Congruence on Members' Decisions to Publicize Votes

The geographic congruence between district boundaries and media markets is measured by a trichotomous variable with values low, medium, and high.[7] Each district was categorized by examining how many media markets covered the district and how many other districts shared its media market(s) (called Areas of Dominant Influence). This serves as a rough measure of the probability that a respondent learned from the news media how his member voted. Table 12 shows the percentage of members who publicized their vote on each issue broken down by level of congruence.[8] For the Use of Force Resolution, the percentage of members publicizing their position decreased significantly as the district/media market congruence increased.[9] While 31.6 percent of members in the low category publicized their vote, none of those in the highest level did so. Members' decisions to publicize their votes on the

1993 Budget-Reconciliation legislation were not as significantly affected by media market congruence. While there is virtually no difference between the behavior of members in the high and medium categories, the percentage of members in the low category who publicized is significantly larger than the percentage in the medium category.[10] The influence of local media outlets on public knowledge of representatives' budget votes was probably mitigated by national news coverage proclaiming that the legislation was opposed by every Republican in the House. Those who were most likely to learn about their member's vote from the local news media probably were informed by national media outlets because of the high level of partisanship displayed in the vote. If district/media market congruence were not important in affecting constituents' knowledge on this issue, then members' decisions about publicizing their vote would not be affected as much by this factor.

Overall, these results suggest that a representative's decision about whether or not to expend the effort to publicize her position will be affected by the probability that her constituents already know how she voted. Since publicity requires the expenditure of resources, a member will refrain from this expense when she feels the need has already been filled. By including the district/media market congruence variable in the model I control for the effect of the local news media on constituents' knowledge. If members are less likely to publicize a vote when they believe their constituents already know it, this would bias my results against finding that publicity efforts have a significant effect.

The 1991 Persian Gulf War Use of Force Resolution

The Persian Gulf War Use of Force Resolution passed the House of Representatives on 12 January 1991, by a vote of 250 to 183. Three Republicans opposed the resolution, while 164 supported President Bush by

TABLE 12. Members Who Publicized Vote for Each Level of Media Market Congruence (in percentages)

	Total	Low	Medium	High
Persian Gulf War Vote	22.9	31.9	17.2	0
($N = 122$)	($N = 28$)	($N = 23$ out of 72)	($N = 5$ out of 29)	($N = 0$ out of 21)
1993 Budget-Reconciliation Vote	41.7	48.4	34.4	34.6
($N = 120$)	($N = 50$)	($N = 30$ out of 62)	($N = 11$ out of 32)	($N = 9$ out of 26)

voting in favor. There was a much more significant split among Democrats. Eighty-six Democrats (32.4 percent) supported the resolution, while 179 voted in opposition. Apart from the vote breakdown, the public rhetoric surrounding this issue was not extremely partisan. Twenty-three percent of the 122 members whose districts were included in the 1991 NES survey publicized how they voted on the resolution. The difference between the parties was not significant, with 21.6 percent of Democrats and 26.3 percent of Republicans publicizing their votes. However, there was a significant difference in behavior between Democrats who supported and those who opposed the resolution.[11] Thirty-seven percent of the Democratic representatives who voted in favor of the resolution publicized their position, while only 11 percent of those who opposed it did so. This occurred because of the overwhelming public approval for the war effort after the conclusion of hostilities.

The percentage of respondents who correctly stated their member's vote was 58 percent, while 30 percent of those who offered a reply were incorrect.[12] Table 13 contains the probit estimates for the effect of the factors on respondents' perceptual accuracy of their representative's vote on the Use of Force Resolution. While all of the results confirm the findings of Alvarez and Gronke (1996), it is the publicity effort variable that we are interested in. As predicted, the model estimates reveal that a respondent whose representative publicized how she voted on the resolution was significantly more likely to have an accurate perception of her position. This demonstrates that members who choose to put forth

TABLE 13. Factors Affecting Respondents' Perceptual Accuracy of Their Representative's Vote on the Persian Gulf War Use of Force Resolution

	Probit Estimate	Standard Error	First Difference
Constant	−0.68*	0.31	—
Media Attention	−0.43	0.21	−4.6%
Political Information	0.72*	0.36	4.4%
Efficacy	−0.11	0.23	—
Education	0.018	0.022	—
Evaluation of Representative	0.01	0.09	—
Partisan Agreement	0.30**	0.10	11.4%
Issue Agreement	0.24**	0.10	9.2%
Issue Salience	0.06	0.10	—
Ideological Extremity	0.18*	0.10	6.7%
Tenure	−0.014**	0.006	−4.2%
District/Media Market Congruence	0.41**	0.14	7.4%
Publicity Effort	0.41**	0.12	14.4%

Note: Percent Predicted Correctly: 64.8 percent. N = 783.
*$p < 0.05$ **$p < 0.01$

the effort can successfully communicate their message to constituents. This is true even for the difficult case in which the information is as specific as a particular vote.

Since these results are probit estimates, first differences are used to gauge the substantive effect of changes in the independent variables on the probability that a constituent provided an accurate response regarding his representative's vote. I calculate the percentage change in respondents' perceptual accuracy resulting from an increase in the independent variable from 0 to 1 for dichotomous variables and from the mean up one standard deviation for others (while holding all other variables at their mean).[13] These results are shown in the last column of table 13. The first difference for the publicity effort variable shows the variance in accuracy between two respondents who are identical in all ways except that one's representative publicized his vote while the other did not. If a member publicized his position on the resolution his constituents were 14.4 percent more likely to be able to accurately state his vote in the survey than if he had not put forth the effort. This substantive effect is the largest of any variable in the model. This is strong evidence that the messages members send can have a big impact on voters' knowledge. If a member has the ability to educate one in seven of his constituents about a specific piece of information that they otherwise would not know, he likely can have an effect on the way he is viewed by a significant proportion of potential voters.

As expected, the estimates show that the level of district/media market congruence had a significant positive effect on a respondent's perceptual accuracy. People living in districts in which the local news media were more likely to provide coverage of the member were significantly better able to accurately state how their representative voted on the Use of Force Resolution. This demonstrates that local news media can have a considerable impact on constituents' knowledge concerning their representative, and this effect can be facilitated or mitigated by the drawing of district boundaries. Computing the first difference for a change in district/media market congruence from the medium to the high category shows a sizable difference in perceptual accuracy. Respondents in high-congruence districts were 7.4 percent more likely than those in medium-congruence districts to state their representative's vote accurately.

The 1993 Budget-Reconciliation Conference Report

The 1993 Budget-Reconciliation Conference Report was adopted by the House on 5 August 1993, by a vote of 218 to 216. All 175 Republican representatives voted in opposition to this proposal advanced by President Clinton. After much wrangling, arm-twisting, and negotiation, enough Democrats were convinced to support the conference report, and it was adopted by the slimmest of margins. The Democratic split was 217 (84.1 percent) in favor and 41 opposed, with the lone Independent providing the other affirmative vote.

The ANES's 1993 Pilot Study included respondents from 120 congressional districts, 70 represented by Democrats and 50 represented by Republicans. The budget was supported by 87.1 percent of the Democrats in the sample, closely mirroring the vote of the entire caucus. Since no Republicans supported the conference report, there was no question that the members in the sample would reflect the vote of Republicans in the House. The percentage of respondents who correctly stated their representative's vote was 62 percent. This was slightly higher than the 58 percent perceptual accuracy of respondents for the 1991 Persian Gulf War Use of Force Resolution, but the difference was not significant. Incorrect answers were given by 21 percent of respondents.[14] The accuracy rate for constituents whose representative voted in favor of the 1993 Budget-Reconciliation Conference Report was 74 percent, while those whose member opposed the legislation were accurate in only 50 percent of the cases. Despite the fact that only 50 percent of the survey respondents were represented by a member who voted "yes" (nearly identical to the percentage of all members who voted in the affirmative on the legislation), 65 percent of respondents believed that their representative voted in favor of the conference report.

Unlike the results for the Persian Gulf War vote, neither the publicity effort variable nor the district/media market congruence variable was significant for the budget vote. These results suggest that differences between the two issues affected the impact of the publicity efforts measured. The most obvious distinction was that the budget was a much more clear partisan battle. The budget conference report was opposed by every Republican in the House, and this unified partisan stance was a national story. Extensive reporting of this fact by the national news media likely resulted in the attentive public having better information regarding Republicans than Democrats. This hypothesis was confirmed when I estimated the model separately for constituents of Democratic and Republican representatives. The media attention variable was positive and significant only for respondents represented by Republicans; higher media attention did not mean greater accuracy for those represented by Democrats. Thus the news media were partly responsible for raising public knowledge of how Republicans voted, but didn't affect perceptions of Democrats. Attentive constituents, those who are most likely to be affected by their member's publicity efforts, probably already knew how Republicans voted on the budget. Thus Republicans had less of an opportunity to have an influence on constituents' knowledge of their vote. Democratic representatives, on the other hand, still had an audience that was not saturated with information concerning their position.

The probit estimates for the model including only respondents with a Democratic representative are displayed in table 14. Despite the fact that the number of observations drops significantly when respondents represented by Republicans are eliminated from the sample, the publicity effort variable is positive and significant. Unlike Republicans, Democratic members were able to affect their constituents' perceptual accuracy on the budget vote. The district/media market congruence did not have a significant effect on the ability of respondents to accurately state the votes of Democratic or Republican representatives.

The first difference shows that when a Democratic representative publicized his position his constituents were 7.7 percent more likely to be able to correctly state his vote than if he had not put forth the effort.[15] While the substantive effect of a member's publicity effort is only a little more than half as strong for the budget vote as for the war resolution, it is larger than the effect of almost all the other factors (except for political information) in this model. The difference in magnitude between members' abilities to affect their constituents' knowl-

TABLE 14. Factors Affecting Respondents' Perceptual Accuracy of Their Representative's Vote on the 1993 Budget-Reconciliation Conference Report, Democratic Representatives Only

	Probit Estimate	Standard Error	First Difference
Constant	−0.928**	0.405	—
Media Attention	0.352	0.332	—
Political Information	1.265**	0.502	7.8%
Efficacy	0.616**	0.344	4.5%
Education	−0.075	0.319	—
Evaluation of Representative	0.036	0.166	—
Partisan Agreement	−0.122	0.148	—
Issue Agreement	−0.010	0.170	—
Issue Salience	0.120	0.172	—
Ideological Extremity	0.209	0.166	—
Tenure	0.013*	0.009	3.5%
District/Media Market Congruence	−0.247	0.200	—
Publicity Effort	0.217*	0.160	7.7%

Note: Percent Predicted Correctly by Model: 67.2 percent. $N = 361$.
*$p < 0.10$ **$p < 0.05$

edge on these two votes shows that this capability depends on the circumstances surrounding the issue. However, the ability of a member to determine whether or not 8 percent of constituents know something about him is still a significant power in electoral politics.

DISCUSSION

Since these results suggest that the messages measured in mailings have an impact on constituents' perceptions, they support my two suppositions: first, members have a significant ability to strategically communicate information to constituents; second, mass mailings serve as an excellent proxy for members' messages to their districts. If representatives can educate their constituents about their positions on votes, it is likely that they can communicate other messages to their constituents that are not as specific. Evaluations of congressional performance are likely to have an effect because they don't need to be recalled in detail by constituents, and they are often reinforced through repetition. The findings in this chapter thus suggest that constituents are receiving and retaining the messages their representatives send regarding institutional performance. But there is a still a big step from reception to behavioral impact. In the next chapter I examine whether members' messages about Congress have an impact on voting in elections.

6 THE ELECTORAL IMPACT OF MEMBERS' MESSAGES

The House of Representatives made significant progress this year in breaking the deadlock that has gripped Capitol Hill.
—*January 1994 newsletter sent by first-year Democrat Karen Shepherd (UT) who was defeated in general election in 1994*

The 103d Congress has been the most productive in years. "Gridlock" is over.
—*Newsletter sent in early 1994 by fourth-term Democrat George Hochbrueckner (NY) who was defeated in general election in 1994*

Members choose their messages about congressional performance by considering what they believe will best help them achieve their goals. The most important effect that a member seeks through his communication is to increase his own probability of reelection, his primary goal. Having shown in the previous chapter that members have the ability to successfully transmit strategic information to constituents, I next examine the electoral impact of messages regarding congressional performance. This will be a test of whether this communication by members can have the intended impact. Once constituents receive these strategic messages, do they respond in the manner sought by representatives, are they unaffected, or is it possible that they interpret the information in a way that may be undesirable to the sender?

This chapter shows that the messages that representatives send about Congress can have a very significant electoral effect. However, in 1994 the impact was not the one that was intended. Instead, a notable portion of representatives sent strategic messages that had the inadvertent result of *lowering* their probabilities of electoral success. Democrats who displayed loyalty to the institution by sending positive messages about congressional performance hurt their electoral chances when their constituents interpreted these messages through their own biases.

This communication did not induce constituents to look more favorably upon the institution but instead caused them to view their representative less favorably, contributing to historic Democratic losses.

THE IMPORTANCE OF INSTITUTIONAL LOYALTY IN THE 1994 ELECTIONS

The 1994 congressional elections that resulted in the Republicans taking control of the House for the first time in forty years caught almost everyone by surprise. Even more striking to political scientists was the apparent overwhelming significance of national factors in producing the Republican landslide. Public distrust and disapproval of Congress were at historically high levels, and this is believed to have contributed to the results (Alford 2001; Chanley, Rudolph, and Rahn 2001; Richardson, Houston, and Hadjiharalambous 2001). This contradicts the conventional wisdom that congressional elections are determined by local factors, not national ones, and incumbents are supposed to possess advantages that in any given election would protect most of them from losing.

Despite the focus on national factors it is important to consider that there was significant variance in the results. Since not every representative seeking reelection was defeated in 1994—in fact, no sitting Republican lost—the election cannot be explained as a revolt by voters against all incumbents. While the Democrats lost fifty-two seats, there were many Democratic incumbents who were able to win reelection. Low public opinion of Congress was certainly part of the explanation for what happened in 1994, but in order to explain the variance it is essential to examine why some members were hurt by public anger and others were not.

At the time of the election, public approval of Congress was very low. Since voter anger at the institution is largely targeted on majority party representatives who are seen as responsible for congressional actions, Democratic incumbents were the ones who were hurt. This fits with Cox and McCubbins' theory that argues that members of the majority have an incentive to cooperate in order to improve their party's record of success running Congress. But since there was variance in the electoral fates of Democratic members, it is important to consider which representatives would have had a greater likelihood of being hurt by negative public views of Congress. It is those Democrats whose behavior caused them to be perceived by their constituents as loyal to their party and the institution that were likely harmed the most.

While there are many facets of a member's behavior that affect how her constituents view her connection to the institution, one that is often examined is her voting record. The assumption is that members who vote more often with the majority party are perceived to have greater loyalty to the institution. If Congress is viewed negatively, then those members who are seen as loyal are more likely to be viewed negatively. But potentially more important than votes—which are often unknown to constituents—is the perception of loyalty created by the messages that members send to their constituents. Those members who communicate praise for Congress are going to be seen as institutional loyalists, and constituents will likely view them with the same lens as they view the institution. Those who "run against Congress" are more likely to be able to separate themselves from constituents' negative views of the institution. If a member can accomplish this, then the reputation of Congress would be less likely to hurt her. Since I have already shown that there was variance among members in their displays of loyalty to the institution in the 1990s—even within each party—I am able to test the effect of messages sent regarding Congress on representatives' fates in the 1994 election.

Explanations Offered for the Results of the 1994 Congressional Elections

Political scientists have struggled to explain the reasons for the upheaval that occurred in the 1994 congressional elections. Some of the suggestions have included low turnout, mobilization of conservative voters, high public disapproval of Congress, unified government, talk radio, the "Perot factor," candidate quality, public dissatisfaction with Clinton, "angry white males," members' voting records, public dissatisfaction with institutional shortcomings in Congress, public disapproval of budget and other policies, the Republican "Contract with America," key Democratic retirements, and delayed effects of redistricting. Some of these factors address the overall trend, while others attempt to explain the variance in individual races.

Explanations of Factors with National Impact

Hibbing and Tiritilli (2000) claim that public disapproval of Congress proved to be more dangerous to incumbents in 1994 than in any other recent election. Their argument is that unified government was responsible for this. Once the Democrats took the White House while maintaining control of Congress, the American people had one party on which to focus their dissatisfaction with government. Hibbing and Theiss-Morse (1995) argue in *Congress as Public Enemy* that public disapproval of Congress—and the government more generally—is caused by dissatisfaction with both policies and processes (see discussion in chap. 3, this vol.). Hibbing and Tiritilli say, "What we are discussing is not responsibility for a certain policy but rather responsibility for how government is operating and, of course, the perception in 1994 was that it was operating badly" (120). Thus it was not what Clinton or the Democrats tried to do once in office, but simply the fact that they were seen as being in control. Some credit is bestowed upon the Republicans and specifically Newt Gingrich for taking advantage of the circumstances, but most of the responsibility for the Democrats' losses is assigned to the condition of unified government and not any specific policies.

Jacobson (1996) also gives unified government an important role in contributing to what happened to the Democrats in 1994. But Jacobson cites policy proposals as being largely responsible for the public ire that was focused on the Democrats. "Budgetary and other national problems left unresolved by years of partisan stalemate" (70) were laid at the feet of the Democrats in 1993. Being in control of the government meant that they could not pass on the blame and had to face the responsibility for developing solutions. Jacobson claims that the Democrats hurt themselves when they asked the American public for the necessary sacrifices to solve the problems facing the country. In addition, Clinton compounded his party's problems by alienating swing voters, the Reagan Democrats, and much of the largely male Perot constituency, through policies of cultural liberalism and support for NAFTA (the North American Free Trade Agreement).

While Jacobson offers a more detailed and variegated explanation for what occurred in 1994, including considering the effects of policy proposals, he does not leave any room for autonomy on the part of individual Democratic members. All of the variance in outcomes cannot be explained by the partisanship of district voters (as measured by the vote in the previous two presidential elections). Some Democrats who should have lost according to this explanation did not, and some who should not have lost did so. It is not the case that national forces completely determined the outcome of all congressional contests. Given the context of past research on congressional elections that suggests that these races are determined by local forces (which are to a large extent controlled by the incumbent), any national explanations that allow representatives virtually no control are inadequate.

Explanations Considering Variation in Members' Behavior

Brady, Cogan, Gaines, and Rivers (1996) go beyond general patterns and attempt to explain the variance among members in their electoral fortunes in 1994. Like Jacobson, they focus part of their explanation on the districts in which the Democrats had fared poorly in recent presidential elections. However, they also suggest that the actions of the individual members themselves had an effect. The more a member supported the president with her votes, the more likely she was to be punished by her conservative to moderate constituents. Therefore a member had some control over her own fate through her level of support for the president. The multivariate analysis revealed that—beyond the effect of a challenger's electoral experience—a member's probability of being defeated was negatively related to the 1992 Clinton vote in the district and positively related to the incumbent's voting support for Clinton.

Brady et al. acknowledge the "shaky history in political science" (1996, 363) of scholars looking for a connection between voting records and reelection, but the results from the 1994 election appear to suggest that this was indeed the case. They argue, however, that the potential importance of members' voting records is "not entirely novel" (364). They remind us that in addition to talking about presentation of self and allocation of resources as important facets of members' home styles, "Fenno added 'explaining Washington activity,' confirming that members do worry that floor votes can come back to haunt them" (364).

While Brady et al. demonstrate the impact that representatives' votes had on their 1994 reelection probabilities, the invocation of Fenno raises a further question. After all, when Fenno described members' "explanations of Washington activity" he was claiming that it is not just what members do in Washington that is significant but how they explain it back home. Thus the analysis of the 1994 election should not end with examining members' votes on particular pieces of legislation. It is essential to look at whether explanations to constituents had an impact on the electoral results and if these obviate the apparent effect of voting records.

The reason that displaying loyalty to the institution would have been especially harmful to members in 1994 is obvious from the explanations of the election cited earlier. If a member was being an institutional loyalist and supporting Congress in his communication with constituents, he was encouraging them to see him as closely connected to his party and the institution. This suggests that he had some responsibility for the governmental policies and processes that raised the ire of the public. This is especially true for Democrats in 1994. An institutional loyalist would have been viewed as endorsing not only Congress, but also the majority party and the president—all three entities being seen as closely connected because of unified government.

CONSTRUCTING THE MODEL

Coding of Loyalty

I developed a loyalty index using my coding of members' messages about Congress that were sent in districtwide mass mailings. Just as in the analysis in the previous chapter I do not include messages sent in targeted mailings since these do not have the same wide-ranging effect on district voters. A member who sent positive messages about Congress in a session, using the criteria outlined in chapter 3, was considered to have been a loyalist for that year. A representative who was negative was coded as disloyal. When a member displayed loyalty he was given a +1 for that session, and when he was disloyal by denigrating the institution he was scored a –1. Those who sent no messages about Congress (and the few who sent mixed messages) were coded 0. Each member's loyalty variable was constructed by adding the scores from 1993 and 1994, thus the index ranges from –2 (disloyalty both years) to +2 (loyalty both years).

I will use Democratic Representative Martin Sabo of the Fifth District in Minnesota as a demonstration of my coding of the loyalty variable. In September 1993 Congressman Sabo sent a newsletter that was entirely dedicated to promoting the recently passed economic package. The first sentence at the top of page 1 reads, "After months of intense negotiating, Congress has passed, and the President has signed, an economic package that embraces deficit reduction, spending cuts, tax fairness, and new investment." This was the only districtwide mass mailing sent in 1993 in which the member communicated a judgment of Congress. Because of the clear praise of the institution for passing the economic plan, Representative Sabo's loyalty score was +1 for the first session of the 103d Congress. In the second session (1994) the representative again received a +1 for the messages contained in two newsletters. In a piece of mail sent in March, Sabo again extols Congress for deficit reduction ("economists praise Congressional action on deficit reduction"). In addition, he repeats President Clinton's assertion that this is the "most productive Congress in 30 years" and he discusses eight "major Congressional accomplishments" to support this claim. A July 1994 newsletter commends congressional action on both a local project and the budget deficit. Because of these messages of loyalty in both 1993 and 1994, Representative Sabo was scored a +2 on the loyalty index for the 103d Congress.

Other Variables

Using the loyalty variable along with the other factors described here, I performed a logit analysis with the dependent variable measuring whether or not the member was defeated in the 1994 general election. In addition to the Loyalty Index, I included other variables in the model that may have explained why a representative lost. The independent variables are Institutional Loyalty, Pro-Clinton Index, the Perot Vote in 1992, the Vote for the Incumbent in 1992, and Redistricting. The Pro-Clinton Index is a simple additive scale describing the number of times the member supported the administration's position on ten key proposals that the president lobbied for or against (see appendix F for the list of the votes). The Perot Vote variable is the percentage of the vote Ross Perot received in the member's district during the 1992 presidential election. The Incumbent Vote variable measures the percentage of the district vote received by the member in the 1992 congressional election. The Redistricting variable is dichotomous and measures whether the member's district underwent substantial change as a result of the redistricting process preceding the 1992 election.[1]

RESULTS

The logit estimates for the equation are found in table 15; I provide estimates for all members and for Democrats only. The results that include members of both parties indicate that support for Clinton, major redistricting, and a lower vote total in the previous election are significant predictors of loss in 1994. The vote for Ross Perot in 1992 did not have a statistically important impact on representatives in 1994. The variable of interest testing the impact of members' messages of loyalty was not found to be significant when considering all members. This was expected because it is only Democrats who were likely to be hurt by their suggestions of loyalty.

Next I turn to the results obtained when considering only Democratic representatives. Leaving aside the impact of loyalty messages for a moment, the findings suggest that the fates of Democrats in 1994 were significantly affected by their level of support in the previous election and whether their district had been altered by reapportionment. The vote for Ross Perot in 1992 did not have a statistically important impact on reelection. It is likely that those members who were hurt because they had a higher number of disaffected constituents (as reflected in the Perot Vote variable) had suffered lower vote totals in 1992, and this factor is already accounted for in the model. In regard to the impact of members' behavior, voting support for Clinton does not explain the variance in the electoral fates of Democrats. This suggests that the voting behavior of representatives did not have an impact on whether their constituents rewarded or punished them in 1994.

The behavior that affected whether Democrats were reelected or defeated was the communication of messages evaluating the performance of the institution. It was those members of the majority who were trying to improve constituents' perceptions of their party's record by being positive about congressional performance who were most likely to be hurt in 1994. These representatives were attempting to communicate this message to their constituents to try to improve their reelection chances. Many of these messages apparently were received and had a significant impact on voters' behavior in 1994. The effect, though, was not the one intended. Constituents did not accept the messages as information about the party and the institution, but interpreted the communication as important data about their representative.

The significant impact of Democrats' messages of loyalty on their defeat can be seen in table 16. The effects have been calculated for different levels of the 1992 vote and redistricting since these were the other two significant predictors of reelection. The Clinton Support Index and Perot Vote are held constant at 7 and 18 percent respectively. A highly vulnerable member, one who received only 50 percent in the previous election, who faced major redistricting had only a 13 percent chance of

TABLE 15. Factors Affecting Probability of Defeat in 1994

	All Members		Democrats	
	Coefficient	Standard Error	Coefficient	Standard Error
Constant	13.65	—	15.8	—
Institutional Loyalty	0.47	0.58	1.26*	0.76
Pro-Clinton Index	0.38**	0.02	0.006	0.04
1992 Perot Vote in District	−0.0012	0.09	0.05	0.11
1992 Vote for Incumbent	−0.36*	0.14	−0.38*	0.16
Redistricting	2.53*	1.21	2.92*	1.42

*$p < 0.05$ **$p < 0.01$ (one-tailed test)

losing if he was negative about Congress in both sessions. However, the same representative had about a 96 percent chance of being defeated if he was an institutional loyalist in both years. A highly vulnerable member who did not face a substantially new district had a probability of defeat near 0 if he consistently bashed Congress, but this probability rose to 55 percent if he was a loyalist. Vulnerable members, those receiving 55 percent of the vote, who faced major redistricting saw a sizable increase in the chance of losing, from 2 percent up to 78 percent, if they decided to be positive instead of negative in both sessions. Safe members (60 percent of the vote in the previous election) who were affected by major redistricting saw their chances of losing increase from near zero to 34 percent if they were always loyal instead of always disloyal. This demonstrates the very substantial effect of a Democrat's messages of loyalty on the probability that he lost in 1994. Why, then, did so many members get caught choosing the wrong behavior?

EXPLAINING DEMOCRATS' MESSAGES DURING THE 103D CONGRESS

Keith Krehbiel has argued that representatives do not run with their parties when seeking reelection, as evident in 1994. He cites a memo to Democratic members from President Clinton's pollster (Stanley Greenberg) "advising that those seeking re-election should emphasize their own records rather than link themselves too closely to Mr. Clinton or even their own party" (1998, 220). That is, a Democratic strategist was telling his members to separate themselves from the party and the institution—"run against Congress." While Krehbiel says that "evidence that Democrats heeded this distancing doctrine is easy to find," the analysis of messages sent in 1993 and 1994 presented here indicates that many majority party representatives were not doing this. Greenberg's advice appears to have been very wise since it was specifically

TABLE 16. Probability of Defeat by Loyalty Score (in percentages)

Loyalty Score	No/Minor Redistricting			Major Redistricting		
	Highly Vulnerable	Vulnerable	Safe	Highly Vulnerable	Vulnerable	Safe
−2	0.8	0.1	0.0	13.0	2.2	0.3
−1	2.8	0.4	0.1	34.5	7.3	1.2
0	9.1	1.5	0.2	65.0	21.8	4.0
1	26.1	5.0	0.8	86.8	49.5	12.8
2	55.5	15.7	2.7	95.8	77.6	34.1

those members who attached themselves to the institution through their rhetoric that were most likely to lose. Because savvy politicians usually do not engage in strategic behavior that proves costly to reaching their primary goal, it is instructive to try to understand this conduct.

I examined the data to see whether there were any differences in the factors that were significant in predicting Democrats' displays of loyalty during the 103d Congress as opposed to the 102d and 104th Congresses.[2] The results reveal important variations in the behavior of Democrats in 1993 and 1994 as opposed to the other years. While the District Partisanship Level was a significant predictor of the type of message sent by Democrats in the 102d and 104th Congresses, it was not significant in the 103d. Majority Support Score was a significant predictor of messages in each of the three congresses but had a larger substantive effect in the 103d Congress than it did in the 102d and the 104th. These results suggest that during the 103d Congress Democrats were more likely to follow their own partisanship when choosing messages and did not cater to the aggregate partisanship of their constituents. Instead of fitting their messages to their constituents' views, members were attempting to lead and convince voters that the Democratic Congress was performing well.

My conversations with members lend support to this explanation of the Democrats' downfall in 1994. As one member said, "We are all reflections of our districts; the incumbent will lose when he is not representative of the district." A few Democrats who survived the 1994 election provided additional confirmation of this in interviews. One Democrat claimed that instead of following constituents, members of his party were "trying to lead and push the agenda forward," which was "one of the reasons we lost in '94." When Republicans began turning up the attacks, Democrats responded by coming to the defense of the institution. Another Democratic member said, "Democrats tried to convince their constituents in '93 and '94 that Congress was doing a good job because they were being attacked by the Republicans." When Gingrich was first elected to the Republican leadership in 1989, *Congressional Quarterly* claimed, "Because Gingrich is such a lightning rod for Democratic fire, his presence in the leadership could make it easier to rally Democratic troops" (Hook 1989b, 628). It appears that in responding to Republican attacks in 1993 and 1994 Democrats played directly into the hands of Republicans by tying themselves to the sinking institution.

If Democrats had known that they were likely to be punished by their constituents for displays of loyalty, they would have had an incentive to distance themselves from Congress and denigrate the institution. So why did many representatives maintain this losing strategy of loyalty? It may have been that Democrats assumed that no matter what they said the public would have held them responsible for the actions of Congress. Democrats held unified control of the federal government for the first time in twelve years, and Bill Clinton was attempting major policy changes. If Democratic members believed that it was not possible for them to separate themselves from the institution in the eyes of their constituents, then the best strategy was actively trying to build up the image of Congress. While this may not have been a good strategy—and the results indicate that it wasn't—many Democrats felt that they had little choice.

Another reason that Democrats may have continued their displays of loyalty to the institution in the 103d Congress is that reputations are difficult to transform. Once a member has established an identity with constituents by sending certain messages, he could harm the trust relationship by attempting to significantly change the content of his communication. Even if a member had determined that it was in his best interest to stop being a loyalist and begin "running against Congress," it may have been impractical to attempt to make this change. This is supported by the lack of significant changes in members' messages of loyalty from the 102d to the 103d Congress. Only two Democrats sent a positive message in either session of the 102d and then a negative message in either session of the 103d. Only four Republicans did the opposite from one congress to the next. This continuity of messages suggests that representatives do not find it worthwhile to attempt to change their reputations, whether because of strategic choice or the potential pitfalls of this strategy.

DISCUSSION

The earthquake that shook Congress in 1994 did not bring down all incumbent members, not even all Democrats. The impact was dependent on the reputations that members had built for themselves in the eyes of their constituents. These perceptions were not based on votes cast; instead they were built through the messages communicated by members to their constituents indicating their level of loyalty to the institution. This finding reinforces the importance of the messages members send to their constituents about congressional performance. This communication *is* critically important in shaping constituents' perceptions, and these perceptions can have significant electoral consequences. However, the effect may not be the one representatives intended when strategically choosing their messages.

Thus, the more that Democratic members' explanations to constituents suggested that they were loyal to the institution, the greater the likelihood that they were defeated in 1994. Democrats who were sending positive messages about eliminating gridlock and passing important legislation were attempting to convince constituents that their party was doing a good job running Congress. Many people received these messages but interpreted them differently from what was intended by the sender. Instead of impacting views of how the Democrats performed in running the institution, these messages were seen to reflect on members' views of the institution. While these results indicate that members have a significant ability to communicate their chosen messages about the institution to constituents, they also demonstrate that voters are not fools!

Usually it is assumed that the sender knows what messages to choose, and if he is successful in his communication he is advantaged. However, if voters are sophisticated enough to interpret the messages representatives send them instead of simply accepting the information at face value, the impact of this communication ability is diminished. Studies of congressional communication usually assume not only that members can successfully communicate their strategic messages, but also that constituents will interpret this information as intended. While 1994 was certainly not a typical year for congressional elections, we see that enough voters acted in a sophisticated manner to spoil the strategies of Democratic representatives. These findings demonstrate that members' messages evaluating congressional performance can have a significant impact on elections. However, we must always be careful in interpreting the effect of congressional communication because the representative-constituent connection is complex. We need to look at both sides of this relationship to fully understand representation.

7 A NEW VIEW OF MEMBERS' BEHAVIOR AND THE REPRESENTATIVE-CONSTITUENT CONNECTION

With years of partisan gridlock behind us, many important new laws have been enacted by this Congress.
—New York's First District Representative George Hochbrueckner (D) in 1994 newsletter

This brand-new Congress is off to a fast start. On the first day . . . we passed a number of important reforms to clean up the House.
—New York's First District Representative Michael Forbes (R) in 1995 districtwide mailing

More than twenty-five years after Richard Fenno's groundbreaking work in *Home Style*, we still have much to learn about the content and consequences of members' communication with their constituents and how it impacts representation. The results I present in this book add significantly to our knowledge in three main areas of interest in the study of the legislator-constituent connection. First, members' messages about congressional performance differ from what has been commonly believed; thus we need to adjust our understanding of the incentives that motivate the behavior of representatives, particularly the influence of partisanship. This evidence supports the much-debated congressional party government theories. Second, since members suggest to their constituents a variety of views of congressional operations, we need to change our understanding of the contributions that representatives are making to public opinion regarding the institution. Third, the evidence that members are able to successfully communicate their chosen messages to their constituents, but the public can interpret these in unintended ways, demonstrates a need for further study of the impact of strategic communication on the legislator-constituent relationship.

UNDERSTANDING MEMBERS' BEHAVIOR

The conventional wisdom has been that members believe that the pursuit of their goals is best served by denigrating Congress. That is, no matter the partisanship of the representative and which party is in the majority, a dominant communication strategy for building trust with constituents includes treating the institution as an adversary. I found that some choose this strategic behavior, but only a relatively small group. In fact, about half of the members utilized a markedly different tactic—they ran for Congress by running *with* Congress! This significant variance among members suggests that we need to reconsider the incentives that shape the actions of legislators. I find that the choice of message about congressional performance is explained by a variety of factors including the member's electoral security and personal winning percentage on key votes. But the driving force is partisanship—the member's own partisan attachment and the partisanship of voters in her district. When it comes to choosing messages about the performance of the institution, the behavior of members reveals the strong influence of parties.

This finding provides important support for theories of congressional party government. Specifically, I have found that the promotion of one's party is an important reelection strategy for a significant portion of members of Congress. But it is essential to make clear exactly what these results contribute (and do not contribute) to the debate over the role of parties in Congress. They do not add significantly to the conditional party government theory proposed by Rohde (1991) and forwarded by Aldrich and Rohde (1998) among others. This theory claims that party leaders use a variety of rewards and punishments in order to coerce their reluctant members to support policies agreed upon by most of those in the party. My results are consistent with this idea; after all, if you are sending messages to your constituents supporting the party's actions, you are not fighting against your party on important issues. However, the party rhetoric we see may only reflect individuals' policy preferences and, when aggregated, the relative homogeneity of preferences within each party (although I do include one control for an individual's preferences, the percentage of *Congressional Quarterly*'s key votes that the member's side won). The analysis presented in this book is not an attempt to provide evidence that members are being persuaded to vote with their party when they might otherwise not be inclined to do so. The swaying of votes by party leaders is key to the conditional party government theory because this theory focuses on party discipline for the purpose of achieving policy goals.

These results are very important, however, in affirming a key element of the party government theory that focuses on achieving electoral goals. This theory (as presented in Cox and McCubbins 1993) claims that party members will be encouraged by party leaders (with various carrots and sticks) to cooperate in the legislative arena so that they can build a record of party accomplishments. Each legislative achievement adds to the public reputation of the party and increases the value of the brand name. A popular party label will help candidates to win in the next election. What I find is that members of the majority use their rhetoric to try to convince their constituents that their party is effectively running the institution. They largely do this by giving Congress credit for policies passed, but some representatives also discuss improvements in congressional processes. Members of the minority, not surprisingly, send messages to damage the record of the majority and build up their party's image as a better alternative. This is the type of "running with one's party" that we should expect to see according to the electorally motivated congressional party government theory. My research provides the first strong evidence supporting the claim that members engage in this partisan behavior. Counter to Krehbiel's (1998) claim that legislators do not run with (and often run against) their party in campaigns, I find clear evidence that this type of partisan rhetoric is part of the permanent campaign engaged in by members of the House. While my findings do not address the other key part of the theory—the impact of parties on legislators' votes—now that we have evidence in the electoral arena, proponents of congressional party government theories can more confidently continue their searches for further support in the legislative arena.

These results demonstrate that much more work is needed to understand the role that partisanship plays in influencing all communication by representatives, whether for electoral, policy, or power reasons. In order to bolster the key finding that members promote and run with their party label, more research needs to be conducted regarding the use of partisan rhetoric in other contexts. There are a number of reasons that similar results will be found no matter where we look. First, members need to be consistent in their messages in order to maintain trust. Second, my results demonstrate that the partisan messages in mail do not vary depending on the audience that is being targeted. Third, when communication is measured only by analyzing mail, we see that these messages have significant effects. I would suggest that the first place to look for further support for the electorally motivated congressional party government theory is in the messages sent in paid campaign advertising.

Another important set of research questions involves the influence of party leaders on the messages that their members communicate. The legislators interviewed for this book claimed varying roles that leaders played in affecting their own communication and that of other members. The leadership of both parties in the House (and Senate) put a tremendous amount of time and resources into encouraging their members to communicate messages formulated to advance partisan goals (Lipinski 1999). The fact that leaders so highly value their communication strategies raises a number of issues that should be studied (for a more detailed treatment see Lipinski 2001b). Some of these issues include the amount of cooperation various members give to partisan communication (Sellers 2000, 2002), the impact that these strategies have on policy-making outcomes, and the effect of communication goals on the legislative process (Evans 2001).

One other particularly important question is the time period in which partisan rhetoric about the institution has been and will continue to be the norm in congressional communication. Looking to the future, is this behavior a permanent feature of congressional communication, or is it a product of the close partisan division in the House? Certainly partisanship will be magnified under conditions in which majority control can easily change in the next election. But Republicans were engaged in this strategy before anyone but the most die-hard partisans believed that a Republican takeover was possible. This suggests that barring any other significant changes in the congressional environment, representatives will continue to send messages about institutional performance based to a large extent on partisanship.

Looking to the past, my results, coupled with prior research and an understanding of the changes that have transpired within Congress, suggest that a change occurred between the 1970s when Fenno made his observations and the early 1990s when my data start. Circumstantial evidence implies that the rise in partisan use of rhetoric about congressional performance coincided with the increase in other indicators of partisan cohesion in the 1980s as discussed by scholars such as Rohde (1991). In fact, the timing of my data compared to Fenno's fits very neatly with narratives regarding increases in party cohesion from the depths of the 1970s to the relative heights of the 1990s (that is, high in comparison to most of the past century). However, it is important to point out that while this makes a compelling story, I have not yet put together all of the evidence to clearly back up this claim. There are a few pieces missing. I was not analyzing the same format of communication that Fenno did, but I do not believe that this is a problem (for reasons already cited). The key missing piece is longitudinal data analyzing the same communication method over the past three decades. This would be important to trace exact points of change in strategic behavior. All of this evidence suggests that there was a change in strategic communication behavior that occurred through the 1980s, but I do not yet have incontrovertible evidence of this.

UNDERSTANDING MEMBERS' CONTRIBUTIONS TO PUBLIC OPINION

Public opinion polls indicate that Congress has experienced an increase in its favorability rating in recent years. This has lessened concerns about the institution losing its legitimacy in the eyes of the American people. However, public opinion regarding institutions of government—especially the House of Representatives, which was designed to be the closest to the people—will always be of considerable import to the functioning of the republic. The finding that members are not all running against Congress strikes at the heart of the belief that members are hurting their own institution with the messages that they send. While scholars and commentators in the early 1990s spoke of a Republican plan to gain control of Congress by bringing down public approval of the institution, no one clearly discussed how this partisan strategy fit—or did not fit—with the conventional wisdom that all members run against Congress. The Republican leadership took the individual-level strategy of running against the institution—meaning the other 434 members—and turned it into a partisan strategy of running against the majority who controlled the institution. Not only was the object of the attack changed, but the strategy was also brought to the national level (in addition to the local level). Members were sending these messages in their districts and also conveying them to a national audience. This nationwide communication made the strategy much more visible.

There were two ways that Democrats could have responded to this Republican strategy: they could make the argument to their own constituents that they were not part of the problem (that is, "run against Congress," à la Fenno), or they could embrace the institution and promote its successes. The evidence shows that while in the majority many of the Democrats promoted the institution, and Republicans did the same once they captured control.

Since the inception of the belief that representatives commonly denigrate the institution, scholars have logically assumed that members were at least partially responsible for typically low levels of public approval for the institution. Having found that there is significant variance in legislators' messages—motivated largely by partisanship—how would this partisan strategy impact aggregate public views of the institution differently than the nonpartisan strategy outlined by Fenno? The obvious distinction is between all members attacking the institution versus only members of the minority party using this type of rhetoric. With the partisan strategy, a majority of members are more likely to send positive messages, therefore overall that strategy appears to be more likely to help in developing good public opinion of the institution. But this was not the common view in the early 1990s when the partisan strategy was often cited as being highly detrimental to public approval of the institution. There are two possible reasons for this view. First, it may be that nonpartisan anti-Congress rhetoric only played out in the districts and was largely out of sight of the national media. Or it may be the case that partisan rhetoric is more virulent in its negativity. It is very difficult to make a good comparison of the exact messages that are sent under each of these two types of strategies, but recent attacks on the institution by its members have been noted—at least anecdotally—as being particularly harsh.

At this point all of the information we have regarding the impact of members' messages on public attitudes toward Congress is simply conjecture. Gauging the impact of this rhetoric would be very difficult because it would require taking content analyses of the messages legislators were sending and linking them up with multiple measurements of public opinion in numerous congressional districts. For a scholar with the resources and the patience, it would be very worthwhile to examine the impact of legislators' messages about congressional processes. Such a study would tie this work together with the extensive research conducted by Hibbing and Theiss-Morse (1995, 2002), who found that citizens who believe that members' actions are motivated by a desire to benefit themselves view the institution unfavorably (2002, 237–38).

Over the five years studied here, there was a fairly even split between members who were positive and those who were negative regarding processes. However, there was significant variance through the years, indicating that legislators were reacting to scandals and changes in partisan control. But only a little more than one in ten members communicated messages about congressional processes. In addition, rhetoric regarding processes was more significantly impacted by constituent partisanship than were policy messages, suggesting that members were preaching to the choir. If views of congressional processes are largely responsible for individuals' opinions regarding the institution, perhaps members are not having a large impact because only a relatively small portion are sending relevant messages. A study of this phenomenon would be a very ambitious project, but it would help to reveal even more about public attitudes toward Congress and the unintended consequences of representatives' strategic behavior. For now, my results show that we should no longer take for granted that members are commonly contributing to negative views of the institution, and we have strong expectations concerning which constituents will be receiving positive or negative messages.

UNDERSTANDING CONSTITUENTS' REACTIONS TO REPRESENTATIVES' MESSAGES

Studies of congressional communication often assume—usually implicitly—that members can be successful in getting their messages to constituents. I provide evidence that legislators *can* increase the likelihood that their constituents are able to correctly identify the position they took on a high-profile issue. There are two ways to look at this finding. First, it is unquestionably beneficial for the public to be aware of the actions of their representatives, especially in regard to critical votes. Democratic theory requires that the electorate be informed in order to choose representatives wisely. The rationale used by members of Congress to give themselves the resources that allow them to send messages to constituents is that communication is necessary for maintaining the representative-constituent link. Examples of these resources abound beyond the taxpayer-financed mailings that I look at. Both chambers of Congress have recording studios that members can use to conduct interviews with the news media or to produce informational television shows to be shown on public access cable channels in their districts. All members are given the resources to create and maintain an official webpage that allows them to post large volumes of information (in text, image, audio, and video files) that they want to make available to their constituents at all times. In addition, every representative is allowed to use office funds to pay for trips home to meet with constituents. These resources appear to be working because my findings indicate that representatives *can* keep their constituents informed—*when they want to.*

This is the downside. Members are strategic in the messages that they send. It is not surprising to find that legislators only choose to communicate their voting record on major issues when they believe that educating constituents will help them build trust. When they think that this information will not be viewed favorably by constituents, they will not disseminate it. If members are not using their communication resources to produce well-educated citizens but instead aim to generate constituents who will be more likely to view the representative favorably, should there be changes made to the system?

First we need to turn to the news media. Local news outlets have the greatest potential for informing large numbers of individuals about their representatives' actions. In regard to questions concerning the objectivity of journalists in covering their local legislators, it seems obvious that the news media can provide information in a much less biased manner than members' offices do. But research into local news coverage indicates that these outlets are largely failing to report on representatives and are especially poor at revealing legislative behavior (Vinson 2002). In addition, my findings buttress previous work that demonstrates that constituents are less educated about their representatives when media market and congressional district boundaries are largely incongruent. A lack of congruence creates little incentive for local news media to cover government officials that serve only a portion of their potential audience. It is highly unlikely that the geography of media markets will become an important consideration for state legislators and others who are in charge of creating congressional districts. Instead, computers facilitate greater opportunities to gerrymander districts that become less congruent with media markets. All of this suggests that we cannot rely on the news media to keep constituents informed about their representatives. While I can lend this evidence and my voice to the pleas to local news media to provide better coverage of representatives, it is clear that other incentives weigh more heavily in their decisions.

If we cannot rely on the news media to inform the public on issues that representatives choose to ignore, should the resources that facilitate members' communication be taken away? Since members confer on themselves the wherewithal to communicate, the only way to change this situation would be for a reform movement to pressure Congress to take away the funding. But we must put more careful consideration into the question of whether a more ignorant electorate is better than one that is informed with selective, but truthful, information.[1] In order to make an informed judgment regarding whether the country would be better off with or without official (taxpayer-funded) communication from members, we need to measure not only whether these messages are received but also the impact that they have on the behavior of constituents. The critical effect that members are trying to have is to build the trust of their constituents and ultimately to secure their reelection. Scholars have argued that the communication resources that are provided to members of Congress have significantly aided the incumbent advantage in congressional elections. This not only means that members give constituents information that they know will be well received, but also that these messages result in the production and maintenance of support.

The previous chapter provided strong evidence that representatives do not always accurately predict the reactions of their constituents. In 1994, a significant number of Democratic members were hurt in their reelection bids by the messages that they sent supporting the institution. This demonstrates again that members can inform constituents; in this instance, I show that representatives have the ability to communicate their views regarding congressional performance. But members obviously did not intend for their messages to result in the loss of their seat. Constituents received the messages but did not respond in the manner that was expected. Instead, they interpreted the information they received through their own lenses rather than taking the messages at face value. This suggests a very important lesson—*voters are not fools.* If constituents can be trusted to interpret the messages their representatives send to them, we should see that this communication can have significant value for the public even when it is biased. Had legislators not had the ability to communicate in 1994, constituents might not have had information that wound up being crucial to them when they cast their votes. While I do not believe that this should be the final word regarding the usefulness of providing communication resources to members of Congress, it is worth careful consideration.

CONCLUSION

Both representatives and congressional scholars would do well to heed what happened in 1994. Members need to realize that even when they are able to communicate their strategically chosen messages, constituents are able to place these in a context that may not reflect well on the representative. In 1994 many Democratic representatives were unable to mold their constituents' opinions regarding Congress; rather, they unintentionally shaped voters' views of the representative's relationship with the institution. I do not expect that these findings will cause a widespread reassessment of electoral strategies by incumbents, but it should teach congressional scholars two lessons. First, all conventional wisdom needs periodic reexamination in order to be sure that we correctly understand the current state of affairs. This reassessment has provided us with a more accurate view of not only members' behavior and the incentives that motivate them, but also of the impact that representatives potentially have on public views of the institution. Second, we cannot assume that representatives can communicate messages that fool all the people, all the time. We should not take for granted the effects of legislators' strategies. Analyzing the communication behavior of members is critical because it can help us to understand their motivations. But in order to have a full picture of the importance of congressional communication, we need to measure the impact that these strategies have on the beliefs and behavior of the public. By doing this we will further our understanding of the legislator-constituent link and representation in the U.S. House.

APPENDIX A:
DISTRICTS SAMPLED
AND REPRESENTATIVES

Number of districts per session: 100
(The appearance of two different district numbers indicates a change that occurred due to redistricting prior to the 103d Congress.)

AL 4	Bevill 102-104
AL 7	Harris 102; Hilliard 103-104
AR 1	Alexander 102; Lambert-Lincoln 103-104
AZ 2	Udall/Pastor 102; Pastor 103-104
AZ 3	Stump 102-104
AZ 6	English 103; Hayworth 104
CA 8/9	Dellums 102-104
CA 10/16	Edwards 102-103; Lofgren 104
CA 11/12	Lantos 102-104
CA 17/20	Dooley 102-104
CA 18/19	Lehman 102-103; Radanovich 104
CA 24/29	Waxman 102-104
CA 25/33	Roybal 102; Roybal-Allard 103-104
CA 33/28	Dreier 102-104
CA 28	Dixon 102 only
CA 38/46	Dornan 102-104
CA 40/47	Cox 102-104
CA 35/40	Lewis 102-104
CA 43/48	Packard 102-104
CA 50	Filner 103-104
CO 4	Allard 102-104
CO 5	Hefley 102-104
FL 3	Brown 103-104
FL 17	Meek 103-104
FL 10	Ireland 102; Miller 103-104
FL 11/15	Bacchus 102-103; Weldon 104

FL 18	Ros-Lehtinen 102-104
FL 15/22	Shaw 102-104
GA 1	Thomas 102; Kingston 103-104
GA 3	Ray 102; Collins 103-104
GA 5	Lewis 102-104
GA 6	Gingrich 102 only
GA 8	Rowland 102-103; Chambliss 104
IA 5/3	Lightfoot 102-104
IA 4	Smith 102-103; Ganske 104
IL 3/5	Russo 102; Lipinski 103-104
IL 6	Hyde 102-104
IL 8/5	Rostenkowski 102-103; Flanagan 104
IL 9	Yates 102-104
IL 21/12	Costello 102-104
IL 22/19	Poshard 102-104
IN 2	Sharp 102-103; McIntosh 104
IN 6	Burton 102-104
KS 3	Meyers 102-104
LA 4	Fields 103-104
MA 2	Neal 102-104
MA 5	Atkins 102 only
MA 7	Markey 102-104
MA 10	Studds 102 only
MD 2	Bentley 102-103; Ehrlich 104
MD 4/1	McMillen 102; Gilchrest 103-104
MD 4	Wynn 103-104
MD 7	Mfume 102-104
MI 10/4	Camp 102-104
MI 7/9	Kildee 102-104
MI 12/10	Bonior 102-104
MI 16	Dingell 102-104
MN 1	Penny 102-103; Gutknecht 104
MN 5	Sabo 102-104
MN 8	Oberstar 102-104
MO 1	Clay 102-104
MO 3	Gephardt 102-104
MO 6	Coleman 102; Danner 103-104
MO 9	Volkmer 102-104
NC 1	Clayton 103-104
NC 7	Rose 102-104
NH 1	Zeliff 102-104
NJ 2	Hughes 102-103; LoBiondo 104
NJ 5	Roukema 102-104
NJ 10	Payne 102-104
NY 1	Hochbrueckner 102-103; Forbes 104
NY 2	Downey 102; Lazio 103-104

Appendixes

NY 5/4	McGrath 102; Levy 103; Frisa 104
NY 9/7	Manton 102-104
NY 17/8	Weiss 102 (first session only); Nadler 103-104
NY 11/10	Towns 102-104
NY 12/11	Owens 102-104
NY 19/17	Engel 102-104
NY 20/18	Lowey 102-104
NY 22	Gilman 102 only
NY 32/29	LaFalce 102-104
OH 6	McEwen 102; Strickland 103; Cremeans 104
OH 18	Applegate 102-103; Ney 104
PA 1	Foglietta 102-104
PA 12	Murtha 102-104
PA 18	Santorum 102-103; Doyle 104
PA 22/20	Murphy 102-103; Mascara 104
SD AL*	Johnson 102 only
TN 2	Duncan 102-104
TN 3	Lloyd 102-103; Wamp 104
TN 5	Clement 102-104
TX 3	Johnson 102-104
TX 7	Archer 102-104
TX 9	Brooks 102 only
TX 15	de la Garza 102-104
TX 19	Combest 102-104
TX 21	Smith 102-104
TX 25	Andrews 102-103; Bentsen 104
TX 26	Armey 102-104
UT 2	Owens 102; Shepherd 103; Waldholtz 104
VA 1	Bateman 102-104
VA 4	Sisisky 102-104
WA 1	Miller 102; Cantwell 103; White 104
WA 2	Swift 102-103; Metcalf 104
WA 8	Chandler 102; Dunn 103-104
WI 4	Kleczka 102-104
WY AL	Thomas 102-103; Cubin 104

* "AL" indicates at-large.

APPENDIX B:
CONTENT CODE

In regard to judgments of the institution, even if there are multiple issues mentioned in an article you must determine ONE overall evaluation of the institution.

Member's name _____
State and District number _____

I. What is the piece identification code? (10x - y.z) _____

II. What type of mail is this? If A, B, or C, how is it targeted (UK = unknown)?
____ A. Letter
        Target? ___ UK ___ area ___ issue (identify) _____
____ B. Obviously Targeted
        Target? ___ UK ___ area ___ issue (identify) _____
____ C. Apparently Targeted
        Guess? ___ UK ___ area ___ issue (identify) _____
____ D. Apparently General Audience

1. What is the article identification letter? (A, B, etc.) _____

2. What aspect of congressional activity is addressed? Check one:
____ A. Public *Policy*
____ B. *Internal* Operations
____ C. *Gridlock* or *Both* Internal and Policy

3. What is the evaluation of the institution? Choose *only one*:
____ A. *Negative*
____ B. *Ambivalent* (including Positive and Negative in same article)
____ C. *Positive*

4. What is/are the issue(s) addressed?

APPENDIX C:
SURVEY OF MEMBERS

Survey
Daniel Lipinski, Ph.D. Candidate
Duke University, Department of Political Science

This is an anonymous survey. No responses will be attributed to any particular member. Your responses will only be used for academic purposes. Thank you very much for your time and cooperation.

___ Democrat
___ Republican

Number of terms you have served (including the current term)

1   2   3   4   5   6   7   8   9   10   11   12+

Part A

Do you currently send mass mailings to constituents? By mass mailings I mean any newsletter, letter, questionnaire, meeting announcement, or other mailing which is sent out in a quantity of 500 or more pieces.
___ Yes   ___ No

If yes, approximately how many of each type of mass mailing do you send in a year? (please circle)

districtwide newsletters	0	1–2	3–4	5 or more	
targeted newsletters	0	1–2	3–5	6–10	11 or more
mass-mailed letters	0	1–2	3–5	6–10	11 or more
questionnaires	0	1	2	3 or more	
meeting announcements	0	1 or more			
other _____					

Appendixes

Do you send fewer mass mailings now than you have in the past?
___ Yes   ___ No

If yes, why?
___ changes in franking allowance
___ I don't need to send out as much mail because I am now better known by my constituents
___ constituent opinion suggests that I send less franked mail
___ other _____
___ other _____

Part B

In your mass mailings have you praised or criticized particular public policies passed by Congress?
___ Yes   ___ No

In your mass mailings have you praised or criticized internal activities of Congress such as the way the House is run (for example, House rules, the way the leadership affects consideration of legislation, or congressional campaign financing) or problems at the House bank, post office, or restaurant?
___ Yes   ___ No

Who do you directly criticize or praise? (check all that apply)
___ Congress, the House
___ the majority or minority party
___ specific ideological groups of members
___ others _____

Do you ever talk about "Congress" or "the House" and intend for it to be understood by your constituents as praise or criticism of the majority party?
___ Yes   ___ No

Do you think any other members ever talk about "Congress" or "the House" and intend for it to be understood by your constituents as praise or criticism of the majority party?
___ Yes   ___ No

The conventional wisdom among political scientists is that "members of Congress run *for* Congress by running *against* Congress"—that is, it is electorally helpful for a member to tell his/her constituents that he/she is different from all the other members of Congress and he/she opposes detrimental congressional policies, bad House rules, and untoward activities conducted by other members.

Appendixes

Do you think that it is it always, sometimes, or never electorally helpful for a member of the *majority* party to be negative toward Congress?
___ Always helpful ___ Sometimes helpful ___ Never helpful

Do you think that it is it always, sometimes, or never electorally helpful for a member of the *minority* party to be negative toward Congress?
___ Always helpful ___ Sometimes helpful ___ Never helpful

Do you think that if a voter disapproves of the job Congress is doing he/she is less likely to vote for an incumbent member of the *majority* party or does it not have an effect on voting?
___ Less likely ___ No effect

Do you think that if a voter disapproves of the job Congress is doing he/she is less likely, more likely, or it doesn't affect the likelihood of voting for an incumbent member of the *minority* party?
___ Less likely ___ More likely ___ No effect

Do you think public opinion about the institution affects the ability of Congress to make public policy?
___ Yes   ___ No

If yes, in what ways?

Part C

If you were not in Congress in 1991 skip to Part E.

Did you advertise in your mass mailings how you voted on the Persian Gulf War Use of Force Resolution in 1991?
___ Yes   ___ No

Why did/didn't you advertise your position in the mass mailings?

Did you try to communicate your vote to your constituents in any other way?

___ Yes   ___ No

If yes, how did you try to communicate your vote? (check all that apply)
___ through TV news
___ through radio news
___ through newspapers
___ town meetings
___ other _____

Appendixes

Part D

If you were not in Congress in 1993 skip to Part E.

Did you advertise in your mass mailings how you voted on the Deficit Reduction/Tax Increase Budget in 1993?
___ Yes   ___ No

Why did/didn't you advertise your position in the mass mailings?

Did you try to communicate your vote to your constituents in any other way?
___ Yes   ___ No

If yes, how did you try to communicate your vote? (check all that apply)
___ through TV news
___ through radio news
___ through newspapers
___ town meetings
___ other _____

Part E

What does your party do to help your communication strategies, specifically the content of mass mailings? (check all that apply)
___ nothing
___ suggest specific issues to discuss
___ suggest language to use when discussing certain issues
___ offer whole articles to include (which only require personalization)
___ other _____
___ other _____

Do you ever follow these suggestions?
___ Yes   ___ No

If yes, when do you follow the suggestions and when do you not follow these?

Do you send the same messages in your mass mailings as you do in other types of communication, or do the messages differ because it is a different method of communicating? How do these messages sent in mass mailings differ?

Do you target specific groups with your mailings?
___ Yes   ___ No

Appendixes

If yes, which groups?
___ senior citizens
___ veterans
___ other _____
___ other _____
___ other _____
___ other _____

Why do you send targeted messages?

APPENDIX D:
EXPLANATION OF VARIABLES IN MODEL PREDICTING MEMBERS' MESSAGES REGARDING CONGRESS

Security: A dichotomous variable valued zero if a member is not electorally secure and one otherwise. A member is considered not to be secure if he received 55 percent or less of the vote in his previous primary or general election, or if his district was drastically changed before the 1992 election. (Sources: Duncan 1991, 1993; Duncan and Lawrence 1995)

Majority Support Score: A continuous variable between 0 and 100. For a majority party member this variable is equal to his party unity score. For a minority party representative this variable is equal to 100 minus his party unity score (which is the percentage of party votes on which the representative voted with the majority instead of his own party). (Party unity scores were obtained from *Congressional Quarterly Weekly Report.*)

Party: Valued zero for Democrats and one for Republicans (the one Independent member of the House was not included in the sample and none of the sampled members switched parties during the period examined).

Seniority: The number of the current term the member is serving.

Key Vote Wins: The percentage of "key votes" in the session—as chosen by *Congressional Quarterly*—that the member voted on the winning side.

District Partisanship: A measure of the extent to which the district constituency favors or opposes the majority party in Congress. For every district in each Congress the percentage difference between the Republican and Democratic vote for president in the two previous elections is added up. If the party who received a larger percentage of the presidential vote in the district is the majority (minority) party in Congress then the District Partisanship variable is positive (negative) for that Congress.

APPENDIX E:
EXPLANATION OF VARIABLES IN MODEL PREDICTING RESPONDENTS' PERCEPTUAL ACCURACY OF THEIR REPRESENTATIVE'S VOTE

Variables from American National Election Study Surveys

Media Attentiveness: An additive index from media variables.
Political Information: An additive index following Zaller (1992).
Political Efficacy: An additive index from efficacy items.
Education: The number of years the respondent spent in school.
Evaluation of the Member: Coded 1 for a thermometer score of greater than 60, 0 otherwise.
Partisan Agreement: Scored 1 if respondent and representative are from the same party, 0 otherwise.
Issue Agreement: Scored 1 if the respondent was in favor of (against) the legislation and he perceived the representative to be in favor (against) the legislation, and 0 if there was disagreement.
Salience: A dichotomous variable scored 1 if the respondent believed the issue that was the subject of the legislation was extremely or very important to himself, 0 otherwise.

Other Variables

Ideological Extremity: Coded 2 if the representative was either extremely conservative (0 through 25) or extremely liberal (75 through 100) on the Americans for Democratic Action scale, 1 if the representative was moderate (26 through 74).
Tenure: The number of years the representative had been in office at the time of the vote.
Media Market Congruence: Coded low (0), middle (.5), or high (1) based on the number of districts included in the media market(s) that

Appendixes

cover the district. Generally, 1 to 3 districts (per media market) was high congruence, 4 to 7 districts middle congruence, and 8 or more districts low congruence. The media market information for each district came from *Congressional Districts in the 1980s* (Gottron 1983) and *Congressional Districts in the 1990s* (Preimesberger and Tarr 1993).

Publicity Effort: Coded 1 if the member mentioned his position (on the vote being examined) in at least one mass mailing, 0 otherwise.

APPENDIX F: VOTES DETERMINING PRO-CLINTON INDEX

1993

H Con Res 64	Fiscal 1994 Budget Resolution/Adoption	March 18	A 243-183
HR 1335	Fiscal 1993 Supplemental Appropriations/Rule	March 18	A 240-185
HR 2264	1993 Budget-Reconciliation/Adoption	Aug. 5	A 218-216
H Con Res 170	Somalia Troop Removal/March 31 Deadline	Nov. 9	A 226-201
HR 3400	Fiscal 1994 Spending Cuts and Govt. Restructuring/Penny-Kasich Amendment	Nov. 22	R 213-219

1994

HJ Res 103	Balanced Budget Constitutional Amendment/Passage	March 17	R 271-153
H Con Res 218	Fiscal 1995 Budget Resolution/Instruct Conferees	April 14	R 202-216
HR 3355	Omnibus Crime Bill/Rule	Aug. 11	R 210-225
HR 3355	Omnibus Crime Bill/Conference Report	Aug. 21	A 235-195
HJ Res 416	U.S. Troops in Haiti/Immediate Withdrawal	Oct. 6	R 205-225

Note: A = Approved, R = Rejected

NOTES

Chapter 1

1. The third activity is allocation of personal and office resources.
2. Emphasis in original.
3. In the words of House Speaker Nicholas Longworth in 1925, "We have always been unpopular." Quoted in Durr, Gilmour, and Wolbrecht (1997, 200). It must be noted that public approval of Congress increased significantly in the late 1990s.
4. Cox and McCubbins (1993) specifically focus on building the party's reputation.

Chapter 2

1. Title 39 of the United States Code, Section 3210(a)(6)(E).
2. Campbell, Alford, and Henry (1984) and Niemi, Powell, and Bicknell (1986) demonstrate that higher levels of congruence result in greater constituent knowledge regarding their representatives in the House.
3. Ninety-three of the districts were analyzed through all five years. I examined 7 districts that were first created in 1993 and therefore only look at mail sent in those districts from 1993 to 1995. I chose 7 random districts to analyze in 1991 and 1992 in order to have 100 in my sample for all five years. The list of the 100 districts in the sample for each year and the members who represented them is contained in appendix A.
4. I would like to gratefully acknowledge the help given to me by Jack Dail and Karen Buehler at the Franking Commission.
5. If I had relied on members' offices there would have been many opportunities for bias in the mailings I collected. Not all offices have a good filing system containing the mass mailings that they have disseminated. Even among those that do, some might have chosen to not comply with my request or, worse, to be selective in turning over only certain pieces of mail (presumably those that would appear less "political"). By going directly to the Franking Commission I was able to avoid these problems.
6. For a history and explanation of the congressional franking privilege see Pontius (1995).

7. The formula at the time of this study was three times the single-piece postage rate applicable to first-class mail multiplied by the number of addresses (other than businesses) in the congressional district, times a factor determined each session by the House Oversight Committee. In addition, each member was given an option of switching $25,000 over from office funds to send additional franked mail. These rules governing the franking allowance were in place for all five years that I examined. Prior to this there were limits on the number of pieces that could be sent by each office. Franking money now comes out of each office's total expenses, which allows representatives to choose between spending money on mailings or any other office expense (such as staff salaries—the most salient trade-off evident in my interviews).

8. In my survey 91 percent said that they do.

9. The rules regulating the content include limits on partisan comments, the use of self-references, and the size and number of photos of the member. Non-frankable items include political cartoons, partisan references to past or future campaigns or elections, prominent labeling of a member's picture with the words *Republican* or *Democrat,* holiday greetings, community service activities (because they are not considered part of a member's official duties), grassroots lobbying or the solicitation of support for a member's position on a legislative or community issue, and news releases announcing filing for reelection or campaign schedule. One of the most important regulations, Section 3210(a)(5)(C) of Title 39, prohibits the use of the frank for "mail matter which specifically solicits political support for the sender or any other person or any political party, or a vote or financial assistance for any candidate for any public office."

10. One representative claimed, "I write every word myself in my newsletters." This member also said that he wasn't sure how to feel when one of his constituents complimented him on the "9th grade level" of writing in his newsletters.

11. A copy of the survey can be found in appendix C.

12. My sample contained significantly more Democrats (63) than Republicans (23) because the survey was distributed directly by a Democratic member of Congress to his colleagues. Although the respondents do not constitute a random sample, I have no reason to believe that they are unrepresentative of members in regard to the issue explored in this book. The seniority of the respondents was distributed as follows: first term, 9 respondents; second, 7; third, 17; fourth, 8; fifth, 6; sixth, 4; seventh, 1; eighth, 9; ninth, 4; tenth, 4; eleventh, 5; twelfth, 10; thirteenth or higher, 2.

13. The downside of anonymous responses is that it is impossible to compare what members say and what the content analysis reveals about their actions.

14. Another term used to refer to this type of mailing is *postal patron* because instead of being addressed to specific individuals they are labeled, for example, "POSTAL PATRON—LOCAL—FIFTH CONGRESSIONAL DISTRICT—IOWA." This means that one copy of the mailing is delivered to every household in the district.

15. At the top of page 1 is a masthead with the member's name and picture. The newsletter is folded to try to ensure that the recipient at least sees the member's name and picture when she gets the mailing.

16. Targeted newsletters are more popular than mass-mailed letters, with the former being utilized by 52 percent of members while the latter are sent by 42 percent.

17. The Veterans Administration provides a list of veterans in a district free of charge to every congressional office. According to members in my survey, the only group that is more popular to target than veterans is senior citizens, which is also a relatively easy group of individuals to find. However, in some states it is easier to get information about constituents than in other states. One staff member told me that in Mississippi there are no good state records with residents' names and addresses. The only records are handwritten (and thus often illegible) and cannot be photocopied, only hand-copied in state offices.

Chapter 3

1. Other reasons it is plausible to assume that reelection is the primary goal of members are provided by Mayhew (1974a).

2. The author has heard this simple exchange occur on the House floor between a party leader and a member breaking with his party on a vote.

3. It is important to note that some of the "congressional party government" detractors, particularly Krehbiel (1998), do not consider these to be legitimate theories. While the author acknowledges weaknesses in these ideas as scientific theories, I will use the term *theories*.

4. One-minute speeches occur immediately after the House goes into session almost every day. Members are allowed to speak for one minute on any topic. Morning hour is usually the hour before the House goes into session on Mondays and Tuesdays. Democrats and Republicans have one half-hour block each. Members can speak for up to five minutes. Special Orders occur after the day's legislative business is completed. Special Orders are divided into two sections. The first section is unlimited and is for any member who wants to speak for up to five minutes. The second section is comprised of two two-hour blocks, one for each party.

5. When I asked the question in my interviews I made sure that I explained my definition of processes.

6. The exact question in the survey was: "In your mass mailings have you praised or criticized internal activities of Congress such as the way the House is run (for example, House rules, the way the leadership affects consideration of legislation, or congressional campaign financing) or problems at the House bank, post office, or restaurant?"

7. This statement is making a positive judgment about the current Con-

gress while criticizing past ones. When conducting the content analysis of judgments I only considered the implication for the current congress.

8. All of the coding was done by two research assistants. The intercoder reliability check revealed a high rate of agreement between the coders—94 percent—for the 48 cases that they both analyzed. A case is one session (year) in one district; there were a total of 499 cases in my sample; Representative Weiss (D-NY) died early in 1992, and a vacancy remained for a significant length of time, thus the year he did not complete was not included in the analysis. The reliability was calculated by having both research assistants code all the mail sent in 24 districts over two years, or 48 cases out of 499. Reliability measures were calculated for each of the five different mailing categories (discussed later). For all mailings taken together the coders agreed on 93.8 percent of the cases. The following agreement percentages were calculated for each of the subsets of mailings: districtwide mail, 95.8 percent; targeted mail, 91.7 percent; policy judgments, 97.9 percent; process judgments, 91.7 percent.

9. In a little more than 1 percent of cases members sent positive messages in targeted mail and negative messages in districtwide mail.

Chapter 4

1. More detailed definitions of these variables are contained in appendix D.

2. Party unity voting scores were obtained from *Congressional Quarterly Weekly Report*.

3. For example, consider one member from each party with an average party unity score of 89 percent. The member of the majority will have a Majority Support Score of 89 and the minority party representative will have a Majority Support Score of 11.

4. For the 102d Congress (1991 and 1992) the previous two elections were 1984 and 1988, while for the 103d and 104th Congresses (1993 through 1995) the previous two elections were 1988 and 1992. For the 1992 election I don't include the Perot vote while calculating the District Partisanship variable.

5. Bauer and Hibbing (1989), however, challenged Jacobson's contention.

6. Although it is tempting to place these members in the same category as those who sent no judgments this would be theoretically problematic. There are significant differences between representatives in these two categories. Those who sent mixed messages were less secure, had lower party unity scores, and had a lower winning percentage on key votes. Despite these differences, when members who sent mixed judgments were placed into the same category as those who sent no judgments the model estimates did not change significantly. An alternative method of classifying members would have been to place everyone who sent at least one positive and one negative piece of mail during a session into the mixed category. It makes more sense, though, to place a member in a category that clearly describes most of his messages instead of inappropriately putting him into the mixed category. Running the model with this operationalization resulted in no consequential differences in the factors that were found to be significant predictors.

7. I did not use an event count to examine the number of mail pieces sent with positive and negative judgments because this type of analysis has theoretical and practical problems. Theoretically it does not make sense for one representative to be considered "seven pieces" positive while another is "one piece" positive, because it is not a strictly additive behavior: a member is either loyally supporting Congress with positive messages or denigrating the institution through negative ones. The scarcity of members who sent both types of judgments demonstrates that most members fall into either one classification or the other. In addition, for targeted mail it is not possible to know how many copies of each piece of mail were sent or exactly which constituents were targeted (the number of copies of a mailing piece that are sent out ranges from 500 to more than 250,000). Therefore, the number of different pieces disseminated doesn't directly reveal anything about how many constituents in a district were sent a particular type of message or how many different pieces were mailed to an individual. In regard to districtwide mail, there was not a great amount of variance in the number of pieces sent (see chap. 2). Thus, counting the number of pieces would not have provided much additional information even if it were theoretically desirable.

8. The model fit was excellent with a -2 log likelihood chi-square of 206.58 ($p = 0.0001$). The test for the equal slopes assumption was also good with a chi-square of 10.68 ($p = 0.0988$). This indicates that it is legitimate to assume that the movements from category one (negative) to two (no messages) and from category two (no messages) to three (positive) can be fit by probit functions with the same slopes.

9. The model was also run substituting in the dichotomous variable measuring whether a member is in the majority or minority. This variable has a very high statistical significance ($p < 0.0001$) and substantive significance. This demonstrates that partisanship itself, not just strength of party support, is a key predictor of members' messages. These results are available from the author upon request (dlipinsk@utk.edu).

10. The first difference gives the change in the probability that a member is in a specific category (negative judgments, no judgments, or positive judgments) given a particular change in the independent variable. In order to determine the first differences all other variables are held at their mean while the factor whose substantive effect is being measured is changed. First differences were determined for the following changes in the variable of interest: Security: from 0 to 1; Majority Support Score: from 11 (average unity, minority) to 89.0 (average unity, majority); Key Vote Wins: from 61.0 (mean) to 77.7 (mean plus standard deviation); District Partisanship: from −42 (average, favor minority) to 42 (average, favor majority); while holding all other variables at their mean: Security: 0.71; Majority Support Score: 63.5; Party: 0.35; Seniority: 6.0; Key Vote Wins: 61.0; District Partisanship Level: −3.5.

11. The exact numbers are 60 (13 percent) negative and 176 (37 percent) positive, with 241 (50 percent) sending no messages and 22 mixed.

12. When I used ordered probit to estimate the model, the diagnostics indicated that the method was appropriate and provided a good fit. Score test for

equal slopes assumption: chi-square = 16.63 (p = 0.0107); –2 log likelihood: chi-square for covariates = 158.54 (p = 0.0001).

13. First differences were determined for the following changes in the variable of interest: Security: from 0 to 1; Majority Support Score: from 11 (average unity, minority) to 89.0 (average unity, majority); Key Vote Wins: from 61.0 (mean) to 77.7 (mean plus standard deviation); District Partisanship: from –42 (average, favor minority) to 42 (average, favor majority); while holding all other variables at their mean: Security: 0.71; Majority Support Score: 63.5; Party: 0.35; Seniority: 6.0; Key Vote Wins: 61.0; District Partisanship Level: –3.5.

14. The exact numbers are 51 (11 percent) negative and 152 (32 percent) positive, with 278 (58 percent) sending no messages and 18 mixed.

15. The diagnostics indicate that the use of ordered probit is appropriate, and the model has a good fit. Score test for equal slopes assumption: chi-square = 12.64 (p = 0.0492); –2 log likelihood: chi-square for covariates = 121.19 (p = 0.0001).

16. First differences were determined for the following changes in the variable of interest: Party: from 0 to 1; Majority Support Score: from 11 (average unity, minority) to 89.0 (average unity, majority); Key Vote Wins: from 61.0 (mean) to 77.7 (mean plus standard deviation); District Partisanship: from –42 (average, favor minority) to 42 (average, favor majority); while holding all other variables at their mean: Security: 0.71; Majority Support Score: 62.4; Party: 0.36; Seniority: 6.0; Key Vote Wins: 60.9; District Partisanship: –4.7.

17. The exact numbers are 80 (17 percent) negative and 245 (52 percent) positive, with 151 (32 percent) sending no messages and 23 mixed.

18. The –2 log likelihood indicates a good fit with a chi-square of 187.78 (p = 0.0001), and the equal slopes assumption appears legitimate with a chi-square of 15.16 (p = 0.0191).

19. First differences were determined for the following changes in the variable of interest: Security: from 0 to 1; Majority Support Score: from 11 (average unity, minority) to 89.0 (average unity, majority); Party: from 0 to 1; Key Vote Wins: from 61.0 (mean) to 77.7 (mean plus standard deviation); while holding all other variables at their mean: Security: 0.71; Majority Support Score: 62.9; Party: 0.35; Seniority: 6.0; Key Vote Wins: 61.0; District Partisanship: –4.4.

20. The exact numbers are 53 (10.7 percent) negative and 51 (10.3 percent) positive, with 393 (79 percent) sending no messages and 2 mixed.

21. The –2 log likelihood (chi-square = 66.15; p = 0.0001) and the test for the equal slopes assumption (chi-square = 17.63; p = 0.0072) indicate that this model is a good fit and is appropriate.

22. First differences were determined for the following changes in the variable of interest: Security: from 0 to 1; Majority Support Score: from 11 (average unity, minority) to 89.0 (average unity, majority); Party: from 0 to 1; District Partisanship: from –42 (average, favor minority) to 42 (average, favor majority); while holding all other variables at their mean: Security: 0.700; Majority Support Score: 61.1; Party: 0.37; Seniority: 5.9; Key Vote Wins: 60.6; District Partisanship: –5.8.

23. This was true whether measuring seniority simply by number of terms served, taking the log of terms, or separating members into generations (first term, two to five terms, five to ten terms, and eleven or more terms).

24. If it were possible it would be instructive to examine 1964 as another demarcation line. Many changes occurred in Congress following this election when a number of the Old Southern committee chairmen lost their ability to obstruct landmark legislation favored by the majority of members. However, there are so few members in my sample who were elected before this time that a comparison is not possible using this data.

25. It is important to note that Loomis believed the opposite may be true. He says, "The actions and sentiments of many House members in the 1980s may present a mirror image of what Richard Fenno found in the 1970s: the ubiquitous strategy of members' 'running *against* Congress'" (1978, 227). This is because this post-Watergate group "may desire to build a stronger institution" because they were able to attain "modest levels of satisfaction and pride in individual achievements" (227).

26. The t-test indicates significance at the $p < 0.10$ level for this cohort variable. First differences were calculated for a secure member who was average on all the other variables: Majority Support Score: 61.1; Key Vote Wins: 60.6; District Partisanship: −4.7.

27. The t-test indicates significance at the $p < 0.025$ level for this cohort variable. First differences were calculated for a secure member who was average on all the other variables: Majority Support Score: 61.1; Key Vote Wins: 60.6; District Partisanship: −4.7.

28. It is interesting to note that this Republican complained that members of his party are more difficult to organize because they are so independent. He compared this to Democrats who have experience in party and union organizations and thus find it easier to work together.

29. This member also said that this anger and aggressiveness was so tangible "you can tell just walking in their offices."

Chapter 5

Another version of this chapter appeared in *Legislative Studies Quarterly*, February 2001 (Lipinski 2001a).

1. However, it is generally acknowledged that the public lacks significant knowledge of their representatives' issue positions. Hurley and Hill's (1980) examination of the 1978 NES survey shows that only 44 percent of respondents were willing to rate their member on any of the issues examined. They suggest that members of Congress are at least partially to blame for this when they claim that "the overall level of citizen ignorance . . . may be a function of the more typical candidate behavior of de-emphasizing issue concerns" (443).

2. It is essential to keep in mind that members are giving explanations of explanations; however, the fact that this was an anonymous survey encouraged truthful responses.

3. The coding was done by two research assistants. There were no discrepancies between coders because of the clarity of the content being coded.

4. Survey respondents in districts in which the member only declared her position in mailings targeted to specific groups were not considered to have been sent this message since it is not clear if they were the target of the communication.

5. Any endeavor to create a multilevel variable measuring the intensity of the effort based on the frequency, prominence, or size of publicity statements in mailings would have resulted in unwarranted precision. Many other factors affect these decisions and do not necessarily reflect the level of effort the member put into publicizing the vote through all media.

6. Similarly, Vinson's (2002) examination of the amount of local broadcast and print coverage given to members reveals that media market congruence has a highly significant effect. She also finds that this impact is not countered by weekly papers because they rarely provide any coverage of members.

7. Generally, 1 to 3 districts (per media market) was high congruence, 4 to 7 districts medium congruence, and 8 or more districts low congruence. The media market information for each district was obtained from *Congressional Districts in the 1980s* (Gottron 1983) and *Congressional Districts in the 1990s* (Preimesberger and Tarr 1993).

8. In both samples the percentage of districts contained in each of the media market congruence categories is skewed toward the low end. More than half of the districts are in the lowest congruence category (59 percent for War vote and 52 percent for Budget vote) while about one-quarter fall in the middle group (24 percent for War and 27 percent for Budget). The highest level of congruence is populated by the smallest number of districts for both samples (18 percent for War and 22 percent for Budget).

9. The level of statistical significance for a one-tailed test of difference in proportions is $p < 0.10$ ($t = 1.50$) between the low and medium categories and $p < 0.025$ ($t = 2.00$) between medium and high.

10. The confidence level is $p < 0.10$.

11. The confidence level is $p < 0.01$.

12. The true positive responses were 36 percent of the sample, and the true negatives were 23 percent. The false positives were 16 percent, and the false negatives accounted for 14 percent of the sample. Twelve percent of the sample would not offer even a guess in regard to their member's vote.

13. First differences were determined for an increase in the variable of interest from its mean up one standard deviation for continuous variables or from 0 to 1 for dichotomous variables: Media Attention: from 0.64 to 0.90; Information: from 0.62 to 0.79; Efficacy: from 0.20 to 0.41; Education: from 12.8 to 15.4; Evaluation: from 0 to 1; Partisan Agreement: from 0 to 1; Issue Agreement: from 0 to 1; Issue Salience: from 0 to 1; Ideological Extremity: from 0 to 1; Tenure: from 9.5 to 17.3; Media Congruence: from 0.5 to 1; Publicity Effort: from 0 to 1; while holding all other variables at their mean: Media Attention: 0.64; Political Information: 0.62; Efficacy: 0.20; Education: 12.8; Evaluation of Representative: 0.50; Partisan Agreement: 0.40; Issue Agreement: 0.38; Issue

Salience: 0.63; Ideological Extremity: 0.57; Tenure: 9.5; Media Market Congruence: 0.46; Publicity Effort: 0.17.

14. True positives were given by 36.8 percent of the respondents, while true negative responses constituted 25.0 percent of the sample. False positives, which accounted for 17.2 percent of the sample, were much more prevalent than false negatives, which were only 4.1 percent. The respondents who would not even offer a guess accounted for 16.7 percent of the sample, which was higher than for the Gulf War vote (11.8 percent).

15. First differences were determined for an increase in the variable of interest from its mean up one standard deviation for continuous variables or from 0 to 1 for dichotomous variables: Media Attention: from 0.50 to 0.73; Information: from 0.74 to 0.92; Efficacy: from 0.22 to 0.43; Education: from 0.50 to 0.77; Evaluation: from 0 to 1; Partisan Agreement: from 0 to 1; Issue Agreement: from 0 to 1; Issue Salience: from 0 to 1; Ideological Extremity: from 0 to 1; Tenure: from 8.2 to 16.3; Media Congruence: from 0.5 to 1; Publicity Effort: from 0 to 1; while holding all other variables at their mean: Media Attention: 0.50; Political Information: 0.74; Efficacy: 0.22; Education: 0.50; Evaluation of Representative: 0.55; Partisan Agreement: 0.54; Issue Agreement: 0.60; Issue Salience: 0.53; Ideological Extremity: 0.56; Tenure: 8.15; Media Market Congruence: 0.51; Publicity Effort: 0.33.

Chapter 6

This chapter was developed from a paper coauthored with William Bianco.

1. This variable was obtained from Gary Jacobson, whose assistance I gratefully acknowledge.

2. I reestimated the model using judgments sent in districtwide mailings since these were the only ones used when determining the loyalty index.

Chapter 7

1. Some may doubt the truthfulness of some messages sent by members of Congress, but no clear evidence of such has been presented. I assert that although much of the information presented by members is biased because it is selective, I don't question its validity.

BIBLIOGRAPHY

Aldrich, John H., and David W. Rohde. 1998. The transition to Republican rule in the House: Implications for theories of congressional politics. *Political Science Quarterly* 112:541–67.

Alford, John R. 2001. We're all in this together: The decline of trust in government, 1956–1996. In *What Is It about Government that Americans Dislike?* ed. John H. Hibbing and Elizabeth Theiss-Morse. New York: Cambridge University Press.

Alvarez, R. Michael, and Paul Gronke. 1996. Legislator and constituents: Learning about the Persian Gulf War. *Legislative Studies Quarterly* 21:105–27.

Balz, Dan, and Ronald Brownstein. 1996. *Storming the Gates.* Boston: Little, Brown.

Bauer, Monica, and John R. Hibbing. 1989. Which incumbents lose in House elections: A response to Jacobson's "The marginals never vanished." *American Journal of Political Science* 33 (1): 262–71.

Bianco, William T. 1994. *Trust: Representatives and Constituents.* Ann Arbor: University of Michigan Press.

Born, Richard. 1990. The shared fortunes of Congress and congressmen: Members may run from Congress, but they can't hide. *Journal of Politics* 52:1223–41.

Boucher, Robert L., and Albert D. Cover. 1996. The changing impact of institutional assessments on vote choice in congressional elections. Paper presented at the annual meeting of the American Political Science Association.

Brady, David B., John F. Cogan, Brian J. Gaines, and Douglas Rivers. 1996. The perils of presidential support: How the Republicans took the House in the 1994 midterm elections. *Political Behavior* 18:345–67.

Campbell, James E., John R. Alford, and Keith Henry. 1984. Television markets and congressional elections. *Legislative Studies Quarterly* 9:665–78.

Canon, David T. 1999. *Race, Redistricting, and Representation.* Chicago: University of Chicago Press.

Chanley, Virginia A., Thomas J. Rudolph, and Wendy M. Rahn. 2001. Public trust in government in the Reagan years and beyond. In *What Is It about*

Government that Americans Dislike? ed. John H. Hibbing and Elizabeth Theiss-Morse. New York: Cambridge University Press.

Cook, Timothy. 1979. Legislature vs. legislator: A note on the paradox of congressional support. *Legislative Studies Quarterly* 4:43–52.

———. 1989. *Making Laws and Making News*. Washington, DC: Brookings Institution.

Cover, Albert D. 1980. Contacting congressional constituents: Some patterns of perquisite use. *American Journal of Political Science* 24:125–35.

Cover, Albert D., and Bruce S. Brumberg. 1982. Baby books and ballots: The impact of the congressional mail on constituent opinion. *American Political Science Review* 76:347–59.

Cox, Gary W., and Matthew T. McCubbins. 1993. *Legislative Leviathan: Party Government in the House*. Berkeley: University of California Press.

Davidson, Roger H., and Walter J. Oleszek. 2003. *Congress and Its Members*. 9th ed. Washington, DC: Congressional Quarterly Press.

Davis, Richard. 1987. Whither the Congress and the Supreme Court? The television news portrayal of American national government. *Television Quarterly* 22:55–63.

Duncan, Phil, ed. 1991. *Congressional Quarterly's Politics in America: 1992*. Washington, DC: Congressional Quarterly Press.

———. 1993. *Congressional Quarterly's Politics in America: 1994*. Washington, DC: Congressional Quarterly Press.

Duncan, Philip D., and Christine C. Lawrence, eds. 1995. *Congressional Quarterly's Politics in America: 1996*. Washington, DC: Congressional Quarterly Press.

Durr, R. H., J. B. Gilmour, and C. Wolbrecht. 1997. Explaining congressional approval. *American Journal of Political Science* 41:175–207.

Elving, Ronald D. 1989. Politics of Congress in the age of TV. *Congressional Quarterly Weekly Report*, 1 April.

Evans, C. Lawrence. 2001. Committees, leaders, and message politics. In *Congress Reconsidered*, 6th ed., ed. Lawrence Dodd and Bruce Oppenheimer. Washington, DC: Congressional Quarterly Press.

Fenno, Richard F., Jr. 1973. *Congressmen in Committees*. Boston: Little, Brown.

———. 1975. If, as Ralph Nader says, Congress is "the broken branch," how come we love our congressmen so much? In *Congress in Change*, ed. Norman J. Ornstein. New York: Praeger.

———. 1978. *Home Style: House Members in Their Districts*. Boston: Little, Brown.

———. 1998. "Home style" revisited: A narrative case study of representational change. Paper presented at the Annual Meeting of the American Political Science Association.

———. 2000. *Congress at the Grassroots: Representational Change in the South, 1970–1998*. Chapel Hill: University of North Carolina Press.

Fiorina, Morris. P. 1979. *Congress: Keystone of the Washington Establishment*. 2d ed. New Haven: Yale University Press.

Bibliography

Fiorina, Morris P., and Paul E. Peterson. 2003. *The New American Democracy.* 3d ed. New York: Longman.

Gottron, Martha V., ed. 1983. *Congressional Districts in the 1980s.* Washington, DC: Congressional Quarterly Press.

Hibbing, John R., and Elizabeth Theiss-Morse. 1995. *Congress as Public Enemy: Public Attitudes toward American Political Institutions.* Cambridge: Cambridge University Press.

———. 2002. *Stealth Democracy: Americans' Beliefs about How Government Should Work.* Cambridge: Cambridge University Press.

Hibbing, John R., and Eric Tiritilli. 2000. Public disapproval of candidates can be dangerous to majority party candidates: The case of 1994. In *Continuity and Change in House Elections,* ed. David W. Brady, John F. Cogan, and Morris P. Fiorina. Stanford: Stanford University Press/Hoover Institution Press.

Hook, Janet. 1988. House's 1980 "Reagan robots" face crossroads. *Congressional Quarterly Weekly Report,* 13 August.

———. 1989a. Battle for whip pits partisans against party pragmatists. *Congressional Quarterly Weekly Report,* 18 March.

———. 1989b. Gingrich's selection as whip reflects GOP discontent. *Congressional Quarterly Weekly Report,* 25 March.

———. 1993. House GOP hones a sharper edge as Michel turns in his sword. *Congressional Quarterly Weekly Report,* 9 October.

Hurley, Patricia A., and Kim Quaile Hill. 1980. The prospects for issue-voting in contemporary congressional elections: An assessment of citizen awareness and representation. *American Politics Quarterly* 8:425–48.

Jacobson, Gary C. 1987. The marginals never vanished: Incumbency and competitions to the U.S. House of Representatives, 1952–82. *American Journal of Political Science* 31:126–41.

———. 1996. Divided government and the 1994 elections. In *Divided Government: Change, Uncertainty, and the Constitutional Order,* ed. Peter F. Galderisi with Roberta Q. Herzberg and Peter McNamara. Boulder: Rowman and Littlefield.

Jacobson, Gary C. 2001. *The Politics of Congressional Elections.* 5th ed. New York: Longman.

Jefferson, Thomas. 1955. *The Political Writings of Thomas Jefferson.* Ed. Edward Dumbauld. New York: Macmillan.

Krehbiel, Keith. 1998. *Pivotal Politics: A Theory of U.S. Lawmaking.* Chicago: University of Chicago Press.

Kuntz, Phil. 1992. GOP moderates take a hit in caucus elections. *Congressional Quarterly Weekly Report,* 12 December.

Lipinski, Daniel. 1999. Communicating the party record: How congressional leaders transmit their messages to the public. Paper presented at the Annual Meeting of the American Political Science Association.

———. 2001a. The effect of messages communicated by members of Congress: The impact of publicizing votes. *Legislative Studies Quarterly* 26:81–100.

———. 2001b. The outside game: Communication as a party strategy. In *Communication and U.S. Elections*, ed. Roderick Hart and Daron Shaw. Lanham, MD: Rowman and Littlefield.

Loomis, Burdett A. 1988. *The New American Politician: Ambition, Entrepreneurship, and the Changing Face of Political Life*. New York: Basic Books.

Madison, James. 1987. *The Federalist Papers*. Ed. Isaac Kramnick. London: Penguin Books.

Mangum, Maurice. 1996. The origins of congressional support. Paper presented at the Annual Meeting of the Midwest Political Science Association.

Mayhew, David. 1974a. *Congress: The Electoral Connection*. New Haven: Yale University Press.

———. 1974b. Congressional elections: The case of the vanishing marginals. *Polity* 6:295–317.

Niemi, Richard G., Lynda W. Powell, and Patricia L. Bicknell. 1986. The effects of congruity between community and district on salience of U.S. House candidates. *Legislative Studies Quarterly* 11:187–201.

Parker, Glenn R. 1981. Can Congress ever be popular? In *The House at Work*, ed. Joseph Cooper and G. Calvin Mackenzie. Austin: University of Texas Press.

———. 1986. *Homeward Bound: Explaining Changes in Congressional Behavior*. Pittsburgh: University of Pittsburgh Press.

Parker, Glenn R., and Roger H. Davidson. 1979. Why do Americans love their congressmen so much more than their Congress? *Legislative Studies Quarterly* 4:53–61.

Patterson, Kelly D., and David B. Magleby. 1992. The polls-poll trend: Public support for Congress. *Public Opinion Quarterly* 56:539–51.

Patterson, Samuel C., and Gregory A. Caldeira. 1990. Standing up for Congress: Variations in public esteem since the 1960s. *Legislative Studies Quarterly* 15:25–47.

Pontius, John Samuels. 1995. Franking. In *The Encyclopedia of the United States Congress*, ed. Donald C. Bacon, Roger H. Davidson, and Morton Keller. New York: Simon and Schuster.

Preimesberger, Jon, and David Tarr, eds. 1993. *Congressional Districts in the 1990s*. Washington, DC: Congressional Quarterly Press.

Richardson, Lilliard E., David J. Houston, and Chris Sissis Hadjiharalambous. 2001. Public confidence in the leaders of American government institutions. In *What Is It about Government that Americans Dislike?* ed. John H. Hibbing and Elizabeth Theiss-Morse. New York: Cambridge University Press.

Rohde, David W. 1991. *Parties and Leaders in the Postreform House*. Chicago: University of Chicago Press.

Sellers, Patrick J. 2000. Manipulating the message in the U.S. Congress. *Harvard International Journal of Press/Politics* 5 (1): 22–31.

———. 2002. Winning media coverage in the U.S. Congress. In *Senate Exceptionalism*, ed. Bruce Oppenheimer. Columbus: Ohio State University Press.

Sinclair, Barbara. 1995. *Legislators, Leaders, and Lawmaking: The U.S. House of Representatives in the Postreform Era.* Baltimore: Johns Hopkins University Press.

———. 1999. Transformation leader or faithful agent? Principal-agent theory and House majority party leadership. *Legislative Studies Quarterly* 24: 421–49.

Tidmarch, Charles M., and John J. Pitney. 1985. Covering Congress. *Polity* 27:463–83.

Vinson, C. Danielle. 2002. *Local Media Coverage of Congress and Its Members: Through Local Eyes.* Cresskill, NJ: Hampton Press.

Yiannakis, Diana Evans. 1982. House members' communication styles: Newsletters and press releases. *Journal of Politics* 44:1049–71.

Zaller, John R. 1992. *The Nature and Origins of Mass Opinion.* Cambridge: Cambridge University Press.

INDEX

Aldrich, John H., 5, 102
Alford, John R., 81, 90
Alvarez, R. Michael, 80–81, 84
American National Election Study (ANES), 2, 23, 26, 74, 80, 81, 82, 84, 86

Bacchus, Jim, 38
Balz, Dan, 27
Bereuter, Doug, 78
Bianco, William T., 75
Bicknell, Patricia L., 81
Born, Richard, 23
Boucher, Robert L., 26
Brady, David B., 93
Brownstein, Ronald, 27
Brumberg, Bruce S., 6
Budget vote (1993), 38, 74–76, 78–80, 82–83, 85–88
Bush, George H. W., 43, 63, 77, 78, 83–84

Caldeira, Gregory A., 3
Campbell, James E., 81
Canon, David T., 11
CBS/*New York Times* poll, 28
Chanley, Virginia A., 90
Class of: 1974, 58–60; 1978, 60; 1980, 60; 1994, 58
Clinton, Bill, 63–64; 1994 voter anger with, 91, 92, 93, 94, 96, 97. *See also* Budget vote (1993)

Cogan, John F., 93
Collins, Cardiss, 78
Commission on Congressional Mailing Standards. *See* Franking Commission
Conditional party government, 102. *See also* Rohde, David W.
Congress as Public Enemy (Hibbing and Theiss-Morse), 35, 92
Congressional approval rating: effect on members' reelection, 23–31, 90, 91–92, 105–6; effect on policy-making, 21–22, 30–31; members' effect on, 4, 20–31, 105–6
Congressional party government theories, 3–4, 5, 8, 24–25, 32, 41–42, 69, 90, 102–3
Congressional Quarterly, 50, 98
Conservative Opportunity Society, 60
Contract with America, 28, 39, 91
Cook, Timothy, 2, 3, 4, 10, 20
COS. *See* Conservative Opportunity Society
Costello, Jerry, 34
Cover, Albert D., 6, 26, 49
Cox, Gary W., 4, 5, 24, 25, 90, 103
CQ. See *Congressional Quarterly*
C-SPAN, 26

Davidson, Roger H., 3, 20
Davis, Richard, 2

Index

Democratic National Committee, 62
Dingell, John, 68
DNC. *See* Democratic National Committee
Dreier, David, 37
Durr, Robert H., 4

Elving, Ronald D., 43
Evans, C. Lawrence, 104

Federalist Papers (Madison), 2
Fenno, Richard F., Jr., 1, 2–5, 6, 9, 19, 20, 22–23, 24, 29, 32, 45, 48, 49, 50, 66, 93, 101, 104, 105–6. See also *Home Style* (Fenno)
Fields, Jack, 33–34, 77
Fiorina, Morris P., 1, 3
Flake, Floyd, 77
Foley, Tom, 63
Franking Commission, 11–12
Franking privilege, 1, 29, 125n. 6, 126nn. 7, 9
Frisa, Dan, 37, 39

Gaines, Brian J., 93
Gilmour, John B., 4
Gingrich, Newt, 27–28, 43–44, 60, 65–66, 92, 98
Greenberg, Stanley, 97–98
Gridlock, 38–39, 40
Gronke, Paul, 80–81, 84

Hadjiharalambous, Chris Sissis, 90
Hefley, Joel, 37
Henry, Keith, 81
Hibbing, John R., 27, 35–36, 91–92, 106
Hilliard, Earl, 38
Home Style (Fenno), 4–5, 50, 101; method used in, 6, 9; "running against Congress" finding, 2–3, 20, 45, 66
Hook, Janet, 28, 60, 65, 98
Horn, Steve, 78
Houston, David J., 90

Internet, 10

Jacobson, Gary C., 6, 30, 49, 92, 93
Jefferson, Thomas, 2

Kleczka, Gerald, 34
Krehbiel, Keith, 5, 25, 32, 97, 103
Kuntz, Phil, 65

Levy, David, 36
Lipinski, Daniel, 26, 27, 61, 104
Loomis, Burdett A., 58

Madigan, Edward R., 27–28
Madison, James, 2
Magleby, David B., 4
Mail. *See* Mass mailings
Mangum, Maurice, 23
Market-district congruence, 10, 81–83, 85, 86–87, 108
Mass mailings, 9–15; defined, 9; rules regulating, 11–12, 29, 126nn.7, 9; targeting, 13–15, 33–34, 44–46, 52–55
Mayhew, David R., 1, 2, 49
McCubbins, Matthew T., 4, 5, 24, 25, 90, 103
Media markets, fit with congressional districts. *See* Market-district congruence
Members of Congress: cohort effects, 58–60; electoral vulnerability effects, 48–49, 52, 53, 55, 56, 66–67; goals of, 2–3, 19–25, 48–49, 52, 75, 102–3; seniority effects, 49–50, 57–60, 67–68
Message types: policy, 35–39, 40–41, 43–44, 55–57, 58–60, 106–7; process, 32–35, 38–39, 40–41, 44, 55–57
Michel, Robert H., 28, 65

National Republican Congressional Committee (NRCC), 65–66
New American Politician, The (Loomis), 58

142

Index

Newsletters. *See* Mass mailings
News media, coverage of Congress and members, 2, 10, 80, 81–83, 85, 86–87, 108; complaints by members about, 37–38
Niemi, Richard G., 81

Oleszek, Walter J., 3
Owens, Major, 37–38

Parker, Glenn R., 1, 4, 20, 49
Party leadership, impact on members' messages, 24–26, 27–28, 61–66, 104, 105
Party record, 5, 24–28, 69, 90, 96, 97–100, 103
Patterson, Kelly D., 4
Patterson, Samuel C., 3
Paxon, Bill, 77
Perot, Ross, 40, 66, 92, 95–96
Peterson, Paul E., 3
Pitney, John J., 10
Powell, Lynda W., 81
Procedural efficiency, 35–36
Procedural equity, 35–36
Public opinion toward Congress. *See* Congressional approval rating

Rahn, Wendy M., 90
Reagan Democrats, 92
Reagan revolution, impact on Republicans' messages, 60
Redistricting (1992), effects of, 40, 91, 95
Representation, 1–2, 107–10
Republican Conference, 61, 65
Richardson, Lilliard E., 90

Rivers, Douglas, 93
Rogers, Will, 63
Rohde, David W., 5, 22, 24, 102, 104
Rohrabacher, Dana, 77
Roukema, Marge, 33
Rudolph, Thomas J., 90

Sabo, Martin, 94–95
Scandals, 36, 37–38, 39–40, 106. *See also* Watergate
Sellers, Patrick J., 104
Senior citizens, as mail target, 14
Sinclair, Barbara, 5
Stark, Pete, 79
Stealth Democracy (Hibbing and Theiss-Morse), 35

Theiss-Morse, Elizabeth, 35–36, 92, 106
Tidmarch, Charles M., 10
Tiritilli, Eric, 27, 91–92
Torricelli, Robert, 78
Towns, Ed, 33, 34–35

Vento, Bruce, 78–79
Veterans, as mail target, 14, 33
Vinson, C. Danielle, 2, 10, 108

Watergate, impact on members' messages, 58–60
Waxman, Henry, 36–37
Wolbrecht, Christina, 4

Yiannakis, Diana Evans, 10–11

Zeliff, Bill, 33